BEATING THE BAT

Beating the Bat

An Autobiography

DEREK UNDERWOOD

Stanley Paul, London

Stanley Paul & Company Ltd
3 Fitzroy Square, London W1

An Imprint of the Hutchinson Publishing Group

London Melbourne Sydney Auckland
Wellington Johannesburg Cape Town
and agencies throughout the world

First published 1975

Set in Monotype Plantin

Printed in Great Britain by Flarepath Printers Ltd
St Albans, Herts, and bound by Wm Brendon & Son Ltd
Tiptree, Essex

ISBN 0 09 123750 5

To my mother and father, brother Keith and wife Dawn for their help, support, encouragement and understanding through the bad times as well as the good.

CONTENTS

Photograph Acknowledgements

The author and publisher acknowledge the following for permission to reproduce photographs of which they own the copyright:

Central Press, Croydon Advertiser, Kentish Gazette, Kent Messenger, Patrick Eager, Rex Features, Sport and General, Universal Pictorial Press.

1. A SCHOOLBOY'S DREAM

The elusive wicket of Gary Sobers . . . a cricketing family . . . early teachers . . . With Kent Second Eleven.

It took me almost nine years to get my man. When I finally numbered him among my 1000 plus victims, the score was nought for plenty. That does not take into consideration a dislocated finger and a split finger, in addition to the hours of humiliation resulting in bruised and battered bowling figures. Yet the memory of those dark and often miserable moments through the years was swept aside in one blinding moment of pure ecstasy out in the middle on the picturesque Queen's Park Oval, Trinidad, during the month of February, 1974.

I needed the cooperation of Mike Denness to spring the trap and take the wicket I had been waiting for since 1966. Mike doesn't miss much in the field. Yet, for a moment, I couldn't help wondering whether my man was going to escape again as the ball sped towards mid-on. Then Mike's hands closed around it momentarily, before hurling the ball towards the heavens as if in a gesture of thanks. By then the batsman was already on his way back to the pavilion.

Two months later, on the same ground, he was mine again. This time I did not need the help of anybody else. I held the ball back a little as the batsman went to drive, but he misjudged the length. He played over the top of the ball and back went his off stump. A pained look immediately spread over his face as he turned slowly and then headed back to the pavilion to make what will probably be his last long walk in Test cricket. This time it was made in a stunned silence, a contrast to the noise and applause which had usually accompanied him when he had walked to and from the wicket in his previous ninety-two Test appearances for his country.

Yes, Gary Sobers was his name. The greatest all-round cricketer I have seen. The finest ever in the view of most others whose memories stretch back to cover many playing years before I was born, and who have witnessed some of the other 'greats' whose names mean nothing more to me than entries in record books, followed by a list of achievements which may occupy only a few lines but speak volumes of their ability.

The first time I captured the wicket of Sobers meant a lot to me personally. I had made my Test debut against the West Indies at Trent Bridge in 1966 when Sobers was captaining the side. Since then I had fought countless battles with him when playing against the West Indies, the Rest of the World and Nottinghamshire without once being able to claim his wicket in a first class contest.

I had been forced to wait until the West Indies' first innings of the opening Test match in Trinidad to even things up a little. At the time, however, my moment of joy hardly warranted more than just a passing mention in reports. It was just another Test wicket.

Looking back on the way I felt on that occasion it is hard to imagine I could have reaped even greater satisfaction when getting his wicket for a second time. Yet I did. Others shared that golden moment with me. The rest of the England team for a start. We saw the departure of Sobers in the final Test at Trinidad as the removal of the last obstacle between us and the restoration of our pride.

Having been beaten in the first Test, coming bravely from behind to draw the next two, and seeing the fourth washed out, we desperately needed victory in the final game to emerge from three months in the Caribbean with our heads held high. Geoff Boycott set up the chance with innings of 99 and 112. Tony Greig turned a dream into reality with his thirteen wickets in the match. Before we could claim victory, however, we all feared that the obstinacy of Deryck Murray, playing on his home wicket, coupled with the skill of Sobers, might snatch it from us. Even when the West Indies had lost five for 85 on that final day towards the 226 they needed for victory.

Those fears increased when Sobers and Murray added exactly

50 for the sixth wicket to reduce the target to 91. It was at that moment I slipped Sobers my slower ball. The final corner had been turned. Although my one wicket in the match didn't compare with Greig's astonishing thirteen for 156, I still considered it a match-winning contribution: not just the wicket, but my supporting role to Greig in blocking up one end to keep the runs to a minimum.

As it was the West Indies finished only 27 runs short of their target, which would have given them the series two-nil. Another half an hour of Sobers would probably have done it. Instead he became one of the most vital victims of my career. Sobers, the master, was mine. A left-hander, too. And, according to my critics, I'm not supposed to round up too many of that breed.

Taking the wicket of Sobers had been one of those dreams I had lived with as long as I can remember. Far beyond that May day in 1963 when I travelled up to Hull by train to make my first class cricket bow with Kent against Yorkshire as a seventeen-year-old. A very immature, nervous seventeen-year-old at that.

By then Sobers had already been playing Test cricket for ten years. I was only just half way through my second year at Beckenham and Penge Grammar School when Sobers claimed the highest individual score in Test history of 365 not out against Pakistan in Kingston early in 1958. He had already become the most prized scalp in world cricket before I really discovered what my left arm was for.

Why I should be left-handed I don't know. As far as I can discover there is no trace of left-handedness in my family either on my father's side or my mother's. Bowling left-arm just seemed the natural thing for me to do. As natural as batting as a right-hander whenever I walked to the crease.

Joining Kent was the second stage of my cricket education. The first part had started many years before with the family in the back garden of our home in Bromley where I was born, and at Farnborough Cricket Club watching my father Leslie Underwood play every Saturday and Sunday during the summer.

He was a right-arm gentle medium-paced bowler and a dogged batsman. My brother Keith, who is three years older than me, also played for Farnborough. He was a genuine quickie although inclined to be erratic at times. A heart attack forced my father to end his playing days not long after I had started playing for Farnborough. My brother is still going strong.

Keith suffered from asthma all his life until he moved to Scotland, where the air seems to suit him. Another illness forced him to abandon his opening bowling role. Instead he concentrated on his batting and captained Poloc in Scottish League cricket. That Underwood route into the Farnborough side started by my father had become quite well trodden by the time Keith and I had walked along the same path.

Before then my cricketing ambitions had been partly fired by my sports master at Dulwich College prep school. He quite frequently took me to the Oval on a Wednesday afternoon – sports afternoon – to watch Surrey who then had May, Lock, Laker, Stewart and others playing for them, and were in the middle of their record-breaking run of championship victories. Keith and I also popped into the Oval now and again, and I was there in 1953 to see Len Hutton win the Ashes. Little did I realize that one day I would be out in the middle on the same ground fighting for those same Ashes.

In addition to the Farnborough side Keith and I had also played together in another team – the school side. When he was seventeen and in his last year at Beckenham and Penge Grammar School he captained the First. Although I was only fourteen I managed to get into that first team and we shared the opening attack for most of one summer. He was a great influence in helping me take all ten wickets in an innings for the first time in any representative match.

We opened the bowling against Bromley Grammar School and I picked up wickets regularly at one end. Keith was not having any luck at the other end and in any other circumstances would undoubtedly have taken himself off. By then I had taken the first seven wickets and he kept himself on, bowling wide of the stumps, to give me the opportunity of taking the other three.

Although I got all the credit it was, in effect, a joint effort and Keith got into the act when we teamed up effectively on another occasion. This time it was for Farnborough against Deptford. Again we shared the opening attack and rolled Deptford over for nine. He picked up four wickets at a cost of three runs and I took the other six for six runs.

Keith and I were the popular heroes that night with the Farnborough team, but the Deptford side did not think too highly of us. We were both still at school and the Deptford players were so upset at being humiliated by a couple of schoolboys that they preferred not to stay to have a drink after the match.

On another occasion that summer I took all ten wickets playing for Farnborough against Bromley Town. I still have the cricket balls with which I took those wickets among my treasured cricket trophies. I suppose bowling was my strong point, but I still fancied myself a little as a batsman. Especially after making 96 for the school against the staff before my English master decided I had done enough damage and gave me out leg-before four short of my century.

By then I was thinking seriously of trying my luck as a professional cricketer. I'd progressed from Farnborough to the higher standard club cricket played by Beckenham Cricket Club, where I was helped tremendously by Ronnie Bryan who played for Kent between the two world wars and skippered them for a time.

He helped to introduce more variety to my bowling, adding to the accuracy I had learned playing with my brother. Not that Keith really appreciated, at the time, that he was setting down the foundations to my career with Kent and England. Nor did I for that matter. It was simply that Keith, like any other youngster, found batting a joy and bowling a chore when practising in the nets in the back garden or playing in the street.

Being the elder brother – and a size or so larger than I was at the time to back up his claim – he naturally had first choice when it came to batting, leaving me to do the bowling. As I was often the only fielder as well, the tighter and more accurately I bowled at him, the less running about I had to do.

By the time I was fifteen I was beginning to win wider recognition through the Kent Schools Cricket Association, which led to representative games for the Southern Schools against the Midlands and the North. Playing in the same Kent Schools side in 1960 was another youngster who went on to play for England.

But not at cricket. The youngster's name was David Sadler, who was then creating a fine impression as a goal scoring inside-forward with Maidstone United in the Southern League but who later made his name as a defender with Manchester United, winning England honours under Sir Alf Ramsey.

We both came under the influence of George Pope, a Kent schoolmaster who did a tremendous amount of work for schoolboy cricket in the county. I can still picture him now striding around the ground, puffing on a cigarette, as he studied us from all angles when watching a match in progress.

There were not many other boys I played with or against at the time who later became professional cricketers, although the Southern Schools side of 1960 contained three who went to Australia in the winter of 1974–75 to defend the Ashes. In addition to myself there was Alan Knott keeping wicket and Geoff Arnold opening the bowling. Knotty and I played for Kent Schools while Geoff played for London Schools. We've grown up together in the world of cricket. I also got my first taste of touring about that time when I was invited to go on a tour to the West Country with the Association of Kent Clubs' junior side.

It was outside the cricket season however that I was first brought to the notice of Kent. During the winters I travelled to Allders Store in Croydon for coaching under Ken Barrington, John Edrich, Tony Lock and other Surrey players. It was Locky, whose left-arm spin role I was later to fill in the England side, who thought I had some potential and recommended me to Les Todd at Kent – for my batting. My bowling he considered as a bonus!

That was the start of my trials with Kent in 1961 when I came under the close scrutiny of Claude Lewis, Colin Page and Les Ames. Bowling out in the open at Canterbury they must have spotted something Locky missed. Claude, now the Kent scorer and for many years the Kent coach, soon advised me to concentrate on my bowling.

It was in the autumn that year that Kent first asked me to join them. I was still waiting for the results of my G.C.E. examinations and my father wrote back to Les Ames asking for time to think about the offer.

If the examination results were promising enough my father still had thoughts of me continuing my education before turning to cricket. As it was the examination results had no sooner arrived than my father had written to Kent accepting a place for me on their staff for the following summer. As it turned out, I'm not too disappointed those exams were not as successful as my father would have wished.

Some of those trial sessions with Kent in 1961 were conducted in secrecy. My headmaster at Beckenham and Penge Grammar School was not keen on allowing cricket to interfere with school studies. The previous year he had refused permission for one of the boys to have time off to play for Kent Schools. Once or twice I slipped away from school to go to Club and Ground matches by pretending I was ill. Arthur Phebey was in on the secret and I remember him telling me once not to stay out in the sun too long. 'You can't go back to school tomorrow with a tan and claim you were ill in bed,' he told me.

During that summer my headmaster once took me aside and told me: 'You never know what mischief you might get up to in the pavilion on wet days.' I can't imagine what he thought went on inside cricket pavilions, but he was sporting enough to send me a congratulatory telegram when I was first selected for England.

I mentioned that Claude Lewis and Colin Page helped me tremendously when I first joined Kent. I remember playing against Surrey at the Oval, bowling on a wet wicket to Mike Willett. I bowled a long hop which Mike easily dispatched for four, and in front of the other lads Colin, who was captaining the Second Eleven, took me down the wicket and showed me the mark where the ball had pitched. Then he told me: 'On a wet wicket always over-pitch rather than pitch short.'

A simple message. My cricket education had begun in earnest, and what wonderful advice it proved to be.

Another who proved very helpful was Tony Catt, the Kent wicketkeeper who was marvellous with the younger players. He had a way of getting the best out of a bowler, and was always ready with words of advice whenever I came up against experienced professionals who happened to be playing in the opposing Second Eleven side for one reason or another: loss of form, recovering from injury, etc.

One of the clearest memories I have of those days is playing my first Second Eleven match after joining the staff. It was against Hampshire on the Old Dunstonians' ground at Beckenham. 'Butch' White was playing for Hampshire, but it wasn't his pace or his long, bustling run like a runaway train gathering speed which had me staring at him with awe.

That previous winter 'Butch' had been in Pakistan with Ted

Dexter's England side, and had played in two Test matches. In that Second Eleven match he was sporting his MCC touring sweater. It was that which had caught my eye. And set me wondering whether I would ever be lucky enough to have one of my own.

2. EARLY SUCCESSES

My first class debut . . . Yorkshire humbled . . . 100 wickets in a season – twice . . . I win my county cap . . . the wily ways of Peter Richardson.

Ray Illingworth has been a major influence in my cricketing career. That relationship is not just confined to his years as England's captain and as my spinning partner. It goes much further back than that. To the month of May 1963 to be exact, the day I made my first class debut at the age of 17 against Yorkshire at Hull. And Ray became my first victim for Kent.

I could not have wished for a better start. My first match was against Yorkshire, the champion county, containing five Test players plus two others who were to play for England before the year was out. Then a home match against Northamptonshire at Dartford followed by a visit to Middlesex at Lord's, the headquarters of world cricket. I've known players who have been in the game two or three seasons before they have played at Lord's. I got there in my third match.

My start to that season could not have been more impressive either. I was named as Twelfth man for Kent's first match against Somerset down at Taunton. I arrived in a Rolls-Royce. Not mine, I hasten to add. I was driven down by Mr Stuart Chiesman, Colin Cowdrey's father-in-law, who was then chairman of Kent. The County lost a most enthusiastic leader when he died in 1968 when MCC were touring Pakistan.

By the time I arrived in Taunton I already knew that bowling could be a tough, demanding and unrewarding life at times. I'd acted as Twelfth man a couple of times the previous season and watched Kent in one or two other home matches. All my early memories are of batsmen scoring centuries.

I had watched Colin score 103 against Gloucestershire at Gravesend. Then seen Billy Alley, now a Test umpire, take Kent for 155 on the same ground when playing for Somerset. I can also remember Mike Smith of Warwickshire scoring 124 against Kent at Folkestone. My main recollection of that Taunton match in May, 1963, is of Graham Atkinson opening Somerset's innings and making 177. I was wondering what I had let myself in for.

I was given my early chance with Kent following a tragic accident during the summer of 1962 to Dave Halfyard, which put him out of cricket for a long period. He was travelling to Weston-super-Mare in his bubble car, ready to play in a championship match, when he was involved in an accident which left him badly injured. This left Kent short of bowlers for 1963, especially in the slower category.

After my Twelfth man duties against Somerset I returned to Kent to play in a Club and Ground fixture while the first team were at the Oval. Dave Nicholls and I were actually playing when we were both told to leave the match early and meet up with the first team at King's Cross Station for the journey to Hull and the match against Yorkshire. Kent had two injury doubts. I got my chance in place of David Sayer and Nicholls took over from Stuart Leary.

The first day turned out to be an anti-climax with rain washing out play after twenty-five minutes. But it still had its heart-stopping moments for me. When Dave and I arrived at King's Cross we were put in charge of the baggage. When we arrived at the Hull ground the next day, one piece was missing.

It belonged to Peter Richardson, leading the side in place of Colin Cowdrey who missed the start of the summer through injury. In fact I saw little of Colin during my debut season. No sooner was he back playing for Kent than England whisked him away for Test matches against the West Indies—and he was put out of cricket for the rest of that summer after his left arm was broken by a delivery from Wes Hall during that dramatic drawn second Test at Lord's. Actually the injury was not the end of the match for Colin. He still had to come back in that Test as England's last batsman when the final over started with the match still poised to finish in any one of four ways. Both sides still stood a chance of victory, a draw the most likely result, and a tie still a possibility. With Colin, his arm in plaster, at the non-striker's end, David Allen, the Gloucestershire off-spinner, played out the final over to earn a draw.

Peter was not too happy when I told him his case was missing. He was a good captain in Colin's absence and a much changed player when he joined Kent. He had started his career with Worcestershire and earned a reputation as a dogged batsman, but with us he became more of a cavalier. Happily for my relationship with the captain, the lost luggage was not my fault. Peter remembered he had taken it up to his hotel bedroom the previous night and forgotten to bring it down in the morning.

The misery of watching the rain fall on that first day was soon forgotten on the second. Yorkshire continued their first innings and I finished my first full day of championship cricket with four wickets for 40 runs. I admit I was a little fortunate. After the rain it wasn't the worst wicket to bowl on, and the Yorkshire batsmen helped when trying to score quickly to make up for lost time.

That was exactly what Illingworth was doing when he mistimed an attempted drive and offered a simple catch to David Baker, our leg-spinner, at cover. The memory lives with me still. I followed up by bowling Ken Taylor and then saw Fred Trueman and Don Wilson caught in the deep by Nicholls, both batsmen chancing their arm. Illingworth, Trueman and Taylor were all Test players, the first two just having returned from Australia with Ted Dexter's team for the 1962–63 attempt to win the Ashes. Doug Padgett was another Test player in the Yorkshire side along with Brian Close. These two got the top scores for Yorkshire, Padgett making 101 in their 214. I was later to discover that Padgett was one of the finest batsmen I've met on a wicket where the ball was really turning.

The loss of all but twenty-five minutes on that first day resulted in the match being drawn, but that didn't spoil my satisfaction with the game. I had taken four of the last five wickets to fall, which was good enough to keep me in the Kent side for the following game. There I stayed.

I just managed to top 100 wickets by the end of the summer. I was just eighteen then, the youngest player to take 100 wickets in a debut season. The first time I took five wickets in an innings was against Leicestershire at Grace Road, and I doubt whether I have ever taken another five like that. It was a goodish wicket but the ball was swinging, and I took four of the wickets by the batsmen getting caught close to the wicket off little nicks or bat and pad.

That summer I also claimed ten wickets in a match for the first time when we played Surrey at Blackheath. I picked up four for 25 off 29 overs in the first innings and six for 88 in the second. That was a memorable match for two other 'firsts'.

Brian Luckhurst, who had made his Kent debut five years earlier, scored his first championship century with an undefeated 126 in our 359, after Surrey had been bowled out for 166 in their first innings. Surrey made 294 the second time round, leaving us needing 102 to win. We scored the runs in 82 minutes but lost six wickets doing so when Roger Harman, the Surrey left arm spinner, took four wickets in five balls including the hat-trick. From 93 for two we were reduced to 96 for six, and for the first time I experienced the panic that can spread through a dressing-room whenever the completely unexpected happens and victory looks like being snatched away. The players were all pacing up and down, with skipper Richardson pleading with each batsman as he disappeared through the door, 'Get your head down, we're throwing it away.'

Harman was making a rare Surrey appearance that summer, and he looked a wonderful spin prospect the following year when he took 136 wickets, but he gradually disappeared from the first class game over the following two seasons. He might well have been one of my greatest rivals.

Reaching my 'ton' that summer was a great scramble at the end. At one stage I did not think I was going to make it. I entered the last match against Gloucestershire at Gloucester needing another six wickets. Rain marred much of the first day and washed out the second. When we turned up at the ground for the final day's play of the summer I was still two short.

I had managed four on the first day when Gloucestershire were bowled out for 105. In an effort to make up time Peter Richardson declared our first innings closed the moment we took the lead on the final day which gave me my chance. I did not have long to wait. I shared the opening attack with Alan Brown and dismissed both openers, Arthur Milton and Ron Nicholls, to reach the magic three figures. Later I added another wicket.

But the day was not a happy one for Kent. We bowled Gloucestershire out for 98 in their second innings, which left us needing

95 for victory. We finished seven runs short. There was only 65 on the board when last man John Dye, now with Northants, joined me at the wicket. We put on 22 together before John was stumped. I even managed a six against Sam Cook, which was sufficient to make me the second highest Kent scorer with 20 runs but not enough to give us victory.

Of my 101 wickets in my first season 96 had been taken in the championship. The other five gave me as much pleasure as any apart from those four in my debut game against Yorkshire. They were taken in Kent's other match of the summer against the great West Indies team at Canterbury, in the first innings when the West Indies made 232 for nine declared. Sir Frank Worrell, who had led his side to a 3–1 series victory over England during the previous three months, was my greatest prize. I clean bowled him for five, and this naturally gave me a tremendous thrill. I also accounted for Seymour Nurse and Basil Butcher, and my other two were fast bowlers Charlie Griffith and Lester King. I'd already been in one spot of bother with King and was to be involved in another with Griffith later in my career.

The King incident was completely accidental. It happened during Kent's first innings. I ended up on my backside, legs and arms all over the place, getting out of the way of a beamer. It is not quite the ball an eighteen-year-old newcomer expects in county cricket. Especially from one of the fastest bowlers around at the time. Lester apologized to me immediately and said the ball slipped out of his hand. I believed him. I had done nothing to upset him. It upset me though. My legs were like jelly and he had no trouble knocking back my middle stump next ball. The trouble with Charlie Griffith came later, during my Test debut at Trent Bridge in 1966, the next time I was to meet up with the West Indies. This time it wasn't an accident. But more of that later.

The West Indies match at Canterbury was ruined by the weather on the final afternoon, when it had reached an interesting stage. With Luckhurst scoring 96 and Mike Denness making 80, Kent led by 89 runs on first innings. Peter Richardson declared our second innings closed at 135 for six, leaving the West Indies to get 243 in 195 minutes. They had made 162 for five when the rain came.

Fortunately it held off long enough for me to sample an hour of Worrell, who made 48. It was an arrogant, masterly innings during which he several times cut the ball to the boundary with absolute perfection, both in timing and footwork. In both innings he had been warmly applauded to the wicket, the Canterbury crowd recognizing they were unlikely to see him playing again.

Kent voted me a £50 bonus for taking 101 wickets, but I was looking for something else: not money, but my county cap. I was disappointed when it wasn't awarded to me. I don't think many counties today would have held back if they had found an eighteen-year-old taking 100 wickets in his first season. But perhaps I expected too much.

Instead I had to wait almost another twelve months before Colin handed me my cap. There was a typical Colin touch about the way he gave it to me. None of this quick hand-over in the dressing room and a bare announcement in the newspapers – if somebody remembers to tell the press at all. Winning a county cap is an important step in a cricketer's career. It marks the day he has arrived. The day the county believe he has come to stay and is not just a one or two season wonder. Colin made sure it meant something special to me.

It happened during August 1964, in the middle of Kent's match against the Australians. A day when Canterbury was crowded. I had a feeling something was going to happen because Colin, with great thoroughness, had told my parents the evening before that it might be worth them visiting Canterbury the following day. It was no secret ceremony either. It happened soon after the lunch break when we were in the field. Suddenly Colin held up play, waved in the direction of the pavilion and out came our Twelfth man Mike Denness with my county cap. Colin made the presentation to me on the field with the Australians and a packed Canterbury ground looking on. It was the sort of gesture one had come to expect from Colin. He immediately put me on to bowl.

Three seasons later I experienced the thoughtfulness of the Cowdreys again, this time on my twenty-first birthday. Colin was away at a Test match, while I was playing for Kent at Tunbridge Wells, and his wife Penny took the trouble to drive herself down to present me with the birthday cake she had baked.

The award of my county cap was a signal, I suppose, that I had done enough to convince Colin and Kent of my usefulness.

By then I had also set down a pattern against Yorkshire and Sussex which is still being repeated to this day, for these two sides usually provide me with a hatful of wickets. They certainly did in 1964.

Twelve months after making my first class debut against Yorkshire I found myself inside their county border again, this time at Bradford. Not even the rain could stop us this time. Kent emerged with a 14 run victory with three minutes to spare and I came out with my best bowling figures at that stage. This after we had lost the entire second day to the weather.

The first day had been almost a private duel between Cowdrey and Close after Kent had won the toss. It finished even. Close took six for 29 while Colin held the Kent innings together, scoring 85 of our 249. By the close Yorkshire had made 41 for one. That is how the match stood when the third day started. What a day it turned out to be.

By the way they approached their batting Yorkshire seemed to be going for first innings points as quickly as possible, but they abandoned the chase when I managed to put on the break. In nine overs I bowled six maidens taking two for three, including Close for a duck. It brought a change of tactics with Close declaring three wickets down and 147 runs behind, obviously hoping for a declaration in reply from Colin. He was not disappointed. We increased our lead to 214 whereupon Colin set Yorkshire a victory target of 76 an hour.

Close jumped at the chance and he made sure Yorkshire kept going with an innings of 67 before he was run out. But they were still 14 runs behind when I grabbed the last wicket. In all I got seven for 97, a career best performance, to earn a national newspaper headline the following day: 'Angel babe tames Yorkshire.' It is not among my favourite headlines for its descriptive content. Nor was it strictly true either.

Again I needed the cooperation of Yorkshire batsmen prepared to take every risk in search of runs, as well as the presence of Dave Halfyard at the other end. He was attempting a comeback that summer, having recovered from his car accident 20 months before. We accounted for 44 of the 52 overs Kent bowled during the Yorkshire second innings, and I am sure the Yorkshire policy was to treat the vastly more experienced Halfyard with respect and caution while they attempted to take the runs off me.

That was how it looked when Close hit the first ball he received – I was bowling – back over my head and into the football stand for a gigantic six. That evened up my success in getting him for a duck in the first innings. Nor was that the end. The first ball I bowled to Phil Sharpe also went for six. The same thing happened when I bowled to Fred Trueman. And Ken Taylor's first scoring stroke off me was yet another six, after he had got off the mark with a single. There was no shortage of excitement.

The last hour was played in pouring rain but nobody moved from the ground. There was no thought of any of us on the field making a dash for cover. I might have had another wicket to go along with the seven I captured, for Close offered a sharp chance just as the rain was starting to thicken. It was probably just as well the chance was not accepted. Close, running short of partners, might have called off the hunt there and then. In all, my day's work had brought me nine wickets for exactly 100 runs, and Kent their first victory on Yorkshire soil for twenty-four years.

Beating Yorkshire in those days was the ambition of every county side, especially in front of Yorkshire supporters. After the memory of being presented with my county cap later in that season, the Yorkshire match remains the next high spot of the summer. Yet, in terms of figures, the game a few weeks later against Sussex at Hastings was the more rewarding.

I might have finished with all ten wickets in Sussex's second innings, but had to be content with nine for 28 to improve my career best figures for the second time in the summer. Little Ken Suttle, always a thorn in Kent's flesh, was the batsman who got away. Unlike the Bradford wicket which had been affected by rain, the Hastings pitch was a dry, dusting wicket.

Peter Richardson declared for the second time on the final morning and challenged Sussex to make 300 to win. They got just over the half-way mark. After the heavy roller had been used, the wicket played well for the remainder of the morning and Sussex made good progress scoring 79 for two, Suttle making the most of the conditions by scoring all but 19 of those runs. The two wickets had fallen to me, Les Lenham taken at slip and Richard Langridge caught off bat and pad. During the afternoon, however, the ball began to stop and turn just right for my pace.

I'd changed ends for the afternoon session and started by having Alan Oakman caught behind. Then came Suttle's wicket when he completely misread a good length ball and was bowled. But not by me. David Sayer had interrupted my run to end the threat of Suttle, leaving me to pick up the other six wickets in Kent's 145 run victory.

Unfortunately I missed two of the biggest scalps. Ted Dexter and Jim Parks were both away playing for England against Australia, along with Colin Cowdrey. But the wickets still gave me great satisfaction. They were more than ample revenge for the indignities I had suffered the previous season at the hands of the Sussex batsmen. They had provided the only real black mark of my debut season, which also marked the start of the Gillette Cup competition. We had been drawn against them, the match falling immediately after I had made my first appearance at Lord's in my third championship match.

Suttle had inflicted the pain again. Sussex batted first and made 314 off their ration of overs, with Suttle contributing 104. My contribution to the Sussex score had also been a healthy one. My eleven overs were smashed out of sight for 87 runs. If there has been a worse eleven over return in the competition I've yet to hear of it. Peter Richardson made a brave attempt to steer Kent home, making 124 which still ranks as one of the highest individual innings in the Gillette today, but we were well beaten by 72 runs.

The end of the second season was almost a repeat of the first. The award of my county cap against the Australians had inspired me to a five wicket performance during their first innings, although Tom Vievers spoiled my figures somewhat with a big hitting display.

One more wicket in the Australian second innings left me needing another seven wickets from Kent's final two championship games to reach 100 wickets in a season for the second time. I managed to take five of them in a three wicket defeat by Glamorgan, and it all rested on the final match in the West Country again. Not Gloucestershire this time but Somerset at Taunton, when I was helped by one of the greatest 'strokes' Peter Richardson played in his career. And he pulled quite a few.

By the end of the second day Kent looked booked for an easy defeat. We had been bowled out for 174 despite a century by Luckhurst. Somerset had replied with 215 for three – only one wicket for me making my total 99 – when their acting captain

Bill Alley declared. By the close we had lost five second innings wickets for 91 and it did not look as though Somerset would have much to do on the final day to win the match.

It meant we were only 50 runs ahead by the close of the second day. Four of those wickets had fallen to the left-arm pace bowling of Fred Rumsey, a fairly streamlined bowler in those days and an England player, in an inspired spell. It was then that Richardson played his master-stroke. It was our last evening away from home and we had bought a few bottles of champagne to celebrate. We had a party in the dressing-room before we left the Taunton ground that night. Naturally we had invited Bill Alley along. He's good company.

Both Peter and Bill had sunk a few glasses when Peter pulled Bill to one side and told him:

'You'll ruin everything tomorrow if you open up with Fred again. I'll tell my boys that if you start with Fred we'll block it up. We'll concentrate on staying at the crease and we will not leave you time to get the runs you want in your second innings.'

It was a typical Richardson legpull. But it worked. Instead of facing Rumsey the next morning Richardson and Knott, the two overnight batsmen, faced up to spinners Langford and Kerslake to launch a fine Kent revival. Richardson did not stay all that long but Knotty, Luckhurst, Dixon and myself managed to steer Kent to 247. The last five wickets added 189 and we beat Somerset by 52 runs. Bill had fallen for the legpull and by the time Rumsey came on, Kent were almost safe.

Without the Richardson 'stroke' I doubt whether we would have been able to set Somerset a three figure victory target. That would have meant little chance of me getting a bowl. As it was, I was able to get in eleven overs which was long enough to earn me the wicket I needed to reach 100 for the season.

Richardson was full of jokes of this kind. I fell for one myself earlier that season when we were playing against Nottinghamshire at Trent Bridge. In those days I often wore a Hector Powe suit – I'm still reminded of it these days – which Richardson claimed was the most ill-fitting garment he had ever seen. When we arrived at Nottingham he noticed that opposite our hotel was a Hector Powe shop.

'Be downstairs at nine in the morning in your suit and I'll take you over the road to have it altered so that it fits you properly,'

Richardson commanded me. Like a fool I was pacing the hotel lobby at nine next morning – and still pacing it half an hour later waiting for Richardson. He, of course, was up in his room, chuckling to himself and enjoying his breakfast in bed. Richardson had struck again.

A couple of hours later he attempted another prank. When a Nottinghamshire official asked for the names of the Kent team Richardson gave him the name 'Souchak' instead of Tony Catt as the Kent wicketkeeper, and so it appeared on the giant electric scoreboard which Nottinghamshire boasted at the time. The name of the Kent scorer on the official scorecard was given as 'R. C. Frobisher-Smythe' instead of C. Lewis – another Richardson idea.

There was great amusement as people and reporters came to the Kent dressing-room asking details of Souchak, and Richardson told them all he was an exciting new Kent discovery who had been signed in secret, etc. He gave the most outrageous details.

But that prank backfired though when at least one Nottinghamshire member made an official complaint to the county.

3. MY BOWLING STYLE

Spinner or cutter? . . . 1965, a change of style . . . the 65 over rule . . . Disappointment in Pakistan . . . 'Mean' bowlers and 'wicketbuyers'.

After two seasons of first-class cricket with Kent I had 202 wickets against my name. I had been the youngest player to take 100 wickets in my debut season, the second youngest player in the county's history to be awarded a county cap. Yet already people were beginning to complain that my bowling style and action were not right. They are still saying the same thing today.

So often, in fact, that I have now learned to live with it, yet it upset me at one time. Not that I insist my style is right. I might well have become an even more effective bowler if I had changed. On the other hand, I might easily have destroyed what I have got.

To have become a more orthodox slow left-arm spinner similar to, say, India's Bishen Bedi would have required such a radical change in my bowling action, as well as my approach, that I could only have done it by dropping out of first class cricket for at least a season. And there was no guarantee that I would ever be successful enough to have claimed my place back again.

I have tried to change, many times. More than anybody could imagine. Each time I have ended up returning to the basic style with which I entered first class cricket in 1963 and which has rewarded me with more than 1300 wickets in twelve years. On all types of wickets, home and overseas.

Apart from dropping out of cricket for a season, or switching to right-arm bowling, I do not think I could have done more. I've tried bowling slower and faster. Tried tossing the ball up in the air more. Switched from bowling round the wicket to over the wicket and back again. Attempted to bowl with the umpire standing back as Bedi does. These and so many other ways. *But none of them have been me.* I have not felt comfortable doing any of these things. Yet still many people – even England selectors – feel I should change.

I suppose I have been partly responsible for the criticism. Nobody has ever been quite sure how to describe my bowling. Whenever they have asked me, I have insisted on being classified as a spinner. And that conjures up a picture of a bowler of Bedi's pace and all the other outstanding left-arm spinners before him.

I called myself a spinner because that is how I wanted people to classify me and this is what I am. When bidding for a Test match place I wanted to put myself in competition with other spinners in general and left-arm spinners in particular. Obviously I bowl faster than the average spinner which has led to the difficulty in finding an easy department into which I can be fitted. Looking for an alternative way to describe my bowling, people might have used the term 'cutter' as an easy and simple descriptive word. *But I am not a cutter.*

I am not an orthodox spinner either, and never have been. But I do grip the ball in the same way as the orthodox slow left-arm spinner. Where we differ is that I do not regularly employ flight in an attempt to lure the batsman down the wicket and make him use his feet. Whereas so many spinners such as Pat Pocock, Ray Illingworth and others have suffered, from time to time, with sore and split spinning fingers as a result of being large spinners of the ball, I have escaped this trouble because I have found that with my own particular style I have not had to rely on such a violent finger action in order to make the ball turn.

I use the word 'violent' deliberately because I do give the ball a tweak with my fingers, which is why I say I am not a cutter. At the same time I do employ part of the technique of a cutter by adding to that tweak a dragging motion across the ball as my arm comes over prior to the moment of releasing the ball.

So how should people describe my bowling? It may be a little cumbersome but the most accurate way is 'slow to slow medium left-arm spinner'. That would stop people expecting me to bowl like an orthodox spinner and also make it clear I am not a genuine cutter of the ball like, say, Northamptonshire's Bob Cottam.

I rely on subtle variations of pace for my wicket taking ability allied to bowling a tight line and length, just as any other spinner would do on a good wicket, the difference being that my stock ball is faster than theirs. If the conditions help the ball turn more sharply, then I consider that a bonus. Again just as any spinner would do.

Length and line coupled with the ability to disguise a slower delivery have always been my main assets ever since my school days. Basically I bowled seam up then, when opening the bowling, and concentrated on bowling straight and keeping a good length. More often than not this was sufficient to take wickets at schoolboy level and even at village green level. Moving up a class to play club cricket for Beckenham made me realize I had to do a little extra.

That was the time I added a great variety to my bowling. It was at this stage that Kent began playing a part in my development and Claude Lewis, a left-arm spinner himself, influenced these variations when he told me: 'For every wicket on which you play there is a pace to bowl.'

My stock delivery then was fairly flat and from that I developed a quicker ball, a slower ball, another one slightly slower still, giving it more air, and so on. My bowling remains basically the same today. The one great difference being that I have now become better at adapting my style to different wickets and at exploiting wickets which really give me encouragement.

Early on in my career the former Australian all-rounder turned cricket writer Keith Miller took an interest in my bowling, and he arranged a special session in the middle at Beckenham Cricket Club so that he could bat against me. This was one of the rare occasions he put the pads on again after ending his career as a player. I bowled him – it was probably more a case of him letting me bowl him – with my quicker ball. Several of the lads were watching and ever since that day my faster delivery has been known as the 'Keith ball'.

The difficulty of fitting a bowler into one of the easily defined categories arose again in the West Indies during the MCC tour of 1974 when Tony Greig switched to his slower style after being regarded as a medium paced seamer. Did he become an off-spinner or an off-cutter? Nobody who saw Tony could say one way or the other. Both terms were used to describe his bowling.

Tony certainly regarded himself as an off-spinner, yet, because of the pace with which he bowled, an element of cutting must have been involved.

Far from being a handicap, as some people suggest, the pace of my or Tony's bowling has often proved an advantage on many of the wickets we meet today. Generally wickets everywhere are becoming slower, largely due to Surrey loam being used as a dressing. The slower a bowler bowls, the less margin of error he has on these slow wickets. If the orthodox slow bowler pitches just short of a length, the batsman has more time to position himself to execute the shot. He does not have this amount of time when facing Greig and myself – or somebody like Yorkshire and England's Bob Appleyard of twenty years ago – if we should have pitched on that same spot.

The pace of my bowling resulted in the first attempt to alter my style in 1965. Quite frankly I struggled that summer and finished with only 80 wickets – the only season during my first seven in county cricket that I failed to pass 100 for the summer. For the two previous seasons I had been the new boy in the game. Batsmen were not quite sure what to expect or how to treat me. By my third year they had started to play me with a greater feeling of security, having learned my limitations.

Colin Cowdrey and Les Ames both felt that my pace would be better suited bowling over the wicket, using the angle across the body of the right-handed batsmen to carry the ball away. This meant that I should not have to turn the ball so much and could bowl more towards the slips. I found it difficult and my wicket taking declined in 1965. Colin could see I was worried, and he offered to help me by arranging a special session in the net in his back garden.

My main problem was in adapting the new line I had to bowl from over the wicket and also prevent myself running on the wicket – the latter being a problem with which I am confronted today at times when I bowl over the wicket. I was also criticized in 1965 for bowling far too many down the leg side. The criticism was perfectly justified. When I arrived at Colin's house I found the practice wicket had been laid out with tapes running from end to end a few inches apart. By using the tapes as a guideline and himself acting as batsman, Colin showed me exactly where the ball should pitch to obtain my best line bowling over the wicket. Unfortunately I wasn't very successful in hitting that spot consistently.

Even when I pitched in the right place, producing a normal good length delivery, I found this did not solve the problem. To hit the off stump I had to pitch just outside leg stump allowing for the angle of delivery. If the ball turned in addition I would miss the off stump completely, often by quite a wide margin. The trouble arose with the ball that went with my arm. When it pitched outside leg stump it just carried on down the leg side and any possibility of leg-before decisions in my favour was reduced to a minimum. My arm ball from around the wicket has proved one of my major wicket-taking deliveries.

Another experiment we tried that day was bowling round the wicket, but this time with the umpire standing back. Colin's gardener acted as umpire while I altered my whole approach so that I ran between the umpire and the wicket when I bowled. This seemed unnatural. I had to run in at such an acute angle and then curve my body round the stumps sharply when I bowled. It was so foreign to me that to have continued in this style would have meant changing my whole action completely. This is why I say I would have needed a complete break from first class cricket for at least a season to have mastered a new way of bowling. This was just not on.

The result of that exercise in Colin's back garden was to convince me even more that I was better off bowling at my normal pace round the wicket with the umpire standing up. Bowling round the wicket I could pitch the ball between wicket and wicket – something I had to do in those days to win a leg-before appeal. I could also pitch just outside the off stump and hit the wicket with the ball that went with the arm. And if I pitched off stump or just outside and the ball turned, there was a great chance of finding the edge of the bat. Although the exercise didn't particularly help in any way I was most grateful to Colin for taking the time and effort to advise me.

Despite these lessons I continued to bowl over the wicket in the main during 1965 and was still using this method when I won my first Test cap against the West Indies. My critics who supported the move to get me bowling over the wicket thought they had won their case in that summer of 1966.

They had every justification for thinking that way. In terms of pure figures, 1966 has been my best season. I finished with 157 victims which cost me less than 14 runs per wicket. In addition I was rewarded by being selected for two Test matches against the West Indies. Right from the early matches that summer I was topping the bowling averages, which undoubtedly influenced the England selectors into giving me my first Test opening. Ample evidence, so it was claimed, that bowling over the wicket worked for me.

But I don't think that was the main reason behind my sudden crop of wickets. In 1966 an experiment was carried out limiting to 65 overs the first innings of the first twelve matches one county played against another on a home-and-away basis. As today, no county played all the others twice in the championship. Twelve counties were played twice, and the other four once to make the grand total of twenty-eight played in the championship. Where a county met another county twice in a season, the first meeting between them was played under this new rule aimed to bring about more outright results.

This suited me. The 85-over restriction on first innings, which was continued for a three-year period until 1974, brought complaints that batsmen had no chance of building an innings. In 1966 they had to go even faster. Obviously the opening batsmen were given some time in which to attempt to put down a foundation against the new ball, but this meant the middle order batsmen really had to strike out quickly. Just about the time Colin Cowdrey was introducing me to the bowling attack.

I am convinced this is the reason I reaped such a rich harvest that summer, particularly in the early part of the season when the majority of these 65-over first innings games were played. I can remember one astonishing match in particular when we met Gloucestershire for the first time at Folkestone. I finished up with six for 52 in the Gloucestershire first innings.

It was a nice haul, but not the result of a particularly inspired piece of bowling. Kent had scored 205 runs off 65 overs and, in a desperate attempt to match this score, the Gloucestershire batsmen used the long handle. Of my six wickets no less than five were gained by the trusted Alan Ealham holding catches at deep mid-on. This was a story to be repeated several times that summer. Batsmen got themselves out trying to hit me. It had little to do with me bowling over the wicket.

Not all my wickets came that way. My nine for 37, for instance, against Essex at Westcliff. There was no slogging going on that day. Essex were too preoccupied in trying to make contact, let alone think of hitting the ball. It was the worst wicket on which I've ever had to bowl. In all I took thirteen wickets for 57, and the match came close to finishing in one day. I remember one delivery in particular to Brian Taylor which exploded, hit him on the glove, shoulder, and travelled down to his pads before running onto the stumps.

The match certainly would have been over in one day if we had managed to hold onto a sharp chance offered by Gordon Barker off me early in Essex's second innings. That catch would probably have given me all ten wickets too. It was a remarkable strip, only a couple of yards away from the one on which Essex and Warwickshire had shared almost 1,000 runs for the loss of 30 wickets during the previous three days. The wicket for our match was dry, cracked and dusting. Essex were skittled out for 64 in their first innings. I claimed four for 20 and Alan Dixon picked up three for 17 in six overs.

We did not do all that much better when we batted. Thanks to Stuart Leary chancing his arm now and again for 35, we managed to reach 106 before it was Essex's turn again just after tea. By the close we had them struggling on 53 for seven. Unfortunately the rules do not allow claiming the extra half an hour on the first day. Only Barker was standing firm. He was acting captain in place of Trevor Bailey and determined to set an example to the rest of his side. His was a splendid innings of its type in the conditions.

All those seven second innings wickets down at the close of the first day had fallen to me, so I was still in with a chance of taking all ten when the second day started with Essex only 11 runs ahead. Most of the seven had fallen to catches close to the wicket, and I got number eight on the second morning when Colin Cowdrey held a slip catch to get rid of Tony Jordan. But my chance of all ten disappeared when Alan Dixon nipped in to bowl Ray East, leaving me to take the final wicket of David Acfield. Essex were all out 80 with Barker having carried his bat in a plucky innings of 36.

We were left needing only 39 for victory. Even so we were not too happy about our chances against East, Acfield and Hobbs.

I know Colin was a little apprehensive. We lost our first wicket at 16 and Colin sent Alan Dixon in to bat. I shall always remember him calling to 'Dicko' as he disappeared through the pavilion door: 'Give me a quick six. That would be a great help.' Dicko obliged but was then bowled by Jordan, leaving Denness and Leary to see us to our eight wicket victory.

John Prodger could still not believe the wicket when the match had finished. He wandered out to the middle to have another look at the strip as the groundsman was clearing up the remains. John studied it for a while and then commented sarcastically to the groundsman, 'Nice wicket, that.'

'Thank you,' replied the groundsman. He was convinced there was little wrong with it. In fact he remarked to the cricket writers afterwards: 'Southend Pier is just down the road. It is one and half miles long. And half these batsmen should be taken out and dropped off the end of it.'

By the end of that summer I was ready to return to bowling round the wicket in my normal style, but I still had a go at experimenting on my first representative tour overseas that winter. I had to. I found the conditions the toughest I have ever met when trying to obtain some response from the wicket. But I never succeeded.

The tour was to Pakistan early in January, 1967, with the MCC under-25 party managed by Les Ames and skippered by Mike Brearley, who broke off his studies at the University of California to make a return to first class cricket. It was only a brief return. Fortunately for my peace of mind, the tour lasted only six weeks with three representative matches, one each in Lahore, Karachi and Dacca – now part of Bangladesh.

How I struggled to make any impact. Apart from myself Mike Brearley had the leg-spin of Robin Hobbs and the off-spin of Pat Pocock to call upon. All three of us were vying against each other to be ready to step in if a spinning role became vacant in the full England side. I lost out on the tour. Pocock finished the leading wicket taker with 31 at an average of just over 20. Hobbs was next with 27 at a cost of just over 25 while I was down the list in fourth place with only 13 wickets to show for my efforts. And they cost more than 31 each.

I did everything on that tour to get the ball past the bat, all that Colin Cowdrey and Les Ames had suggested. And more.

But it made little difference. I shared a room with Alan Knott throughout the tour and we spent hours in hotel bedrooms discussing, analysing, dissecting my bowling without finding an answer. It was my first experience of really slow wickets offering nothing in the way of turn or bounce. In the end I just returned to my normal style, the one I use today. I had been picked because I had taken wickets with that style and I reasoned it would be better to stick with it.

There was one heartbreaking moment I shall never forget when I first entered the attack in the opening representative match against Pakistan Under-25 at Lahore. Shafqat Rana was the batsman, a handsome, elegant strokemaker who could have doubled for Omar Sharif as a film star. He had scant respect for any bowler, and I am sure he should have played many more times for Pakistan than he did. The first three balls I delivered to him all went screaming through the covers to the boundary. They had all been a perfect line and length. It was during that innings that I bowled for a two hour spell without once getting the ball through to Knotty behind the stumps!

I suffered two other heartbreaking, mind-shattering moments on that visit, the six unhappiest weeks I have ever spent overseas. The first was against the North Zone at Peshawar, in the match where Brearley scored 312 not out in the day and Knotty scored his maiden first class century. I'm not taking anything away from the performance of these two when I say it was one of the worst first class sides I have ever played against. Thanks to Brearley's effort MCC scored 514 for four on the opening day and the North Zone's bowling really consisted of only Intikhab.

The second day was bad enough, with me emerging from the North Zone first innings with nought for 12 off my five overs while Hobbs took six for 39. But the final day was worse still, when North Zone were fighting against an innings defeat. Hobbs was not quite so effective this time so Brearley brought on Keith Fletcher with his gentle and little used leg-breaks. He took four for 50 and at one stage I honestly felt like packing in the game completely as I stood at cover catching them off Fletch. I did manage one wicket in their second innings: the number eleven batsman who had been out for a duck in the first innings. He had not troubled the scorers in the second when I got his wicket. Which was not altogether surprising. I don't know where the

Pakistan authorities found him but I doubt whether he had been introduced to a bat until shortly before the match started.

It was even worse when we moved to East Pakistan for a two-day game at Chittagong, a warm-up match before the final representative fixture. The night before the match started I had again shared a room with Knotty. It was hot and sticky, and he insisted on sleeping with a huge fan turning all night. Unfortunately for me, the fan was fixed to the ceiling right above my bed. When I woke up in the morning I had a stiff neck and was in no condition to bowl.

I was left out of the match and forced to suffer even more as I watched Alan Ormrod take four for 32 with his off-spinners. It was the first time I realized he turned his arm over! The only consolation for me was that the match was a two-day affair and was not classed as first class.

In the three representative matches – all were drawn – I took only five wickets. I did once get four wickets in an innings on a spinner's wicket in Rawalpindi. That makes nine of the thirteen wickets I took in all. Which is not saying much for my penetrative ability in the other games.

The period between late 1964 and the middle of 1966, plus that six week tour of Pakistan with the MCC Under-25 side, are just two good, healthy reasons why I became so upset whenever critics demanded I should change my style and slow down. I have tried. I don't think I could have done more. But each time I have been forced to revert to my normal style.

These suggestions have come right from the top. On odd occasions Alec Bedser, chairman of England's selectors, has hinted he would like to see me bowl in a slower style. Last season Ossie Wheatley, another selector, suggested I should bowl more from over the wicket as a variation. Brian 'Tonker' Taylor, the former Essex wicketkeeper and captain who became a selector in 1973, is another who tried to help me. He thought my arm was dropping a little and suggested in 1974 that I should try to bowl with a higher arm action. The selectors are probably not aware of my attempts in the past to do all these things and more besides. If I don't put what they say into practice it is not a question of me being rude or ungrateful. It is simply that I have tried them all. I hope they come up with other ideas for I am always willing to listen. Something may come out of discussions. Their advice is a healthy sign, too, of their enthusiasm and desire for us all to be successful.

To change my style of bowling would also require me to change my whole approach to bowling from a mental point of view. I'm a 'mean' bowler rather in the mould of Illingworth. I hate every run that is scored off me. I don't like trying to buy my wickets. I have been forced to on occasions in particular circumstances but I have never been happy doing so. That is just not the way I play the game.

If the wicket is doing something to help me then I want to be in there attacking all the while with the fielders in a catching position. That is bound to leave a few gaps in the field but the batsman has got to be taking a chance trying to hit me into those vacant places. If it is a good, hard, flat wicket then I believe the onus is on the batsman to make the most of it. I'm not going to help him in any way. My job then, as I see it, is to bowl a line and length, keeping everything in check and creating pressure for the batsman. He has got to earn every run he takes off me.

Some spinners, of course, take a different attitude. They will encourage batsmen to hit out hoping they will make a mistake and sky a catch in their enthusiasm. Bishen Bedi, bowling for India against England at Lord's during the second Test match in 1974, was an example. The Indian bowling was slaughtered in that match on one of the best batting strips Lord's had produced for years.

On that occasion Dennis Amiss showed exactly why he had become a world class opening batsman in the West Indies during the winter: he took 188 off the Indian bowlers. Mike Denness chipped in with his first Test century and Tony Greig followed on with 106. The result was an England score of 629 all out. Throughout it all Bedi had worked cheerfully and tirelessly and emerged with six wickets for 226 runs off his 64 overs. He still came up smiling. I would not have done.

My outstanding memory of that match was on the second day, when Mike and Tony were together in their century partnership. Time and time again they were able to push the ball to deep mid-on and deep mid-off for singles. They must have got tired of saying 'Come on' to each other. In the end I don't think they bothered, it was so easy.

I could never have bowled to a field like that. Between them

Bedi and Indian captain Ajit Wadekhar had spread the field out, putting men round the boundary to save the fours. All they succeeded in doing was giving the England batsmen easy runs whenever they wanted them. When Bedi was asked after the match why he didn't attempt to close up the game and make it tighter he replied simply, 'I don't like playing it that way.'

He was tossing the ball up, inviting the batsmen to loft the ball in the air as they went for the big hit. But with all the time at their disposal Denness and Greig were too professional to fall for that trick. They could keep the scoreboard clicking merrily along at four or more runs an over without taking the slightest risk. Bedi's men out in the deep were on the whole completely wasted.

If I had been bowling it would have hurt me to have seen the batsmen taking singles off me when and how they pleased. I believe it is far more important to try to hold the batsmen. When Denness and Greig had settled down and added 30 or 40 together I would have wanted to change my field, but not to the extent Bedi did. I would have wanted a slip with the majority of the rest of the fielders in a ring, pushed back slightly but for the most part near enough to the pitch to make the batsmen think carefully before they attempted to take a single. To beat that field and find the boundary the batsman has either to place the ball accurately along the ground to pass through the gaps in the field, or hit the ball over the top of the ring. Whichever method he adopts he is thus made to work and earn his runs. If he attempts the second course, as many batsmen would in the end when finding their good and orthodox strokes unrewarding, then there is a chance of him making an error of judgement, a chance of a wicket coming the bowler's way.

Bedi did finish with six wickets for his troubles, but three of them were tail end batsmen when England were trying to push the score along towards the end of the second day. And I can't remember any of these batsmen getting caught going for genuine hits over the top – the method by which Bedi was hoping to catch his victims in the field that he had set, or had been set for him.

Whenever I hear the argument put forward that I should slow down and become more of a flight bowler there is one other point I take into consideration. Just how many flight bowlers are there in top international cricket today? Very, very few. Bedi is one, but he was brought up on Indian wickets which helped him. I can't think of many more, certainly not left-arm finger-spinners, who have made it to the top and been successful enough to stay there.

In England Norman Gifford has been my main rival for the left-arm role in the England side. But nobody would call 'Giff' a flight bowler. He may not bowl quite at my pace. His stock ball probably has a little more loop to it than mine. But a flight bowler? Never. Don Wilson of Yorkshire perhaps is one. The reason why Ray Illingworth took him to Australia in 1970–71 was because so many people had raised doubts about my ability to be successful on the Australian wickets. But Don was not successful even with Ray there to set the right fields for him.

Throughout my England career people who are old enough to have seen Yorkshire's great left-arm bowler Hedley Verity in action have compared the two of us. He also bowled faster than the orthodox left-arm spinner during his very successful period with Yorkshire between 1930 and 1939. At the same time he was supposed to have given the ball more air than I do, and many critics have said I should bowl in Verity's style.

But was he any more successful? I don't think so. In 40 Test matches he took 144 wickets. I was four Test matches before him in achieving that 144 total, and bowled far fewer overs. Verity twice toured Australia. The first time in 1932–33 on the famous 'Body-line' tour he took eleven wickets in four Tests, and on his return four years later claimed ten victims in five Test matches. Again my record is better.

Checking on Verity's Test match record I was interested to find an assessment of his bowling by Sir Neville Cardus, one of the most respected cricket writers of the day. Naturally he was full of praise for Verity's bowling in England, but he added: 'Maybe on good pitches his bowling didn't put the question to batsmen which they had to answer when faced with the curving, hovering flights of Rhodes or Blythe.'

That is exactly what people have been writing about me for years. I'm not trying to belittle the figures of Verity, a man who lost his life in the Second World War before I was born. His record of 1956 wickets in ten first class seasons with Yorkshire and England speaks for itself. I'm just trying to point out that although some critics have said I should bowl in Verity's style, our records are similar – taking into consideration the reduced number of championship matches today – and my Test record slightly better. I think I'll stick with my method.

Other people have influenced me to do just that – batsmen out in the middle. Whenever I have discussed my bowling with them the vast majority have said they would prefer me to bowl a little slower and from over the wicket. For the simple reason that they believe they would be able to play me far more easily. The message from these batsmen is simple: 'Stay as you are.'

4. RESERVED FOR WET WICKETS?

What the critics say . . . Pakistan at Lord's, 1974, and India at Old Trafford . . . India again, 1971 . . . Ten Aussie wickets at Headingley, 1972.

I felt sick when I left Lord's after the drawn, washed out second Test against Pakistan in 1974. I felt sick, too, when I was dropped after the drawn Edgbaston Test with which the Pakistan tour opened in 1971. That, too, was ruined by the weather on the last day.

There could not have been a greater contrast between my returns from those two matches. At Edgbaston I had slogged away for the best part of two days while Zaheer Abbas, Asif Iqbal and Mushtaq had all plundered runs on an easy-paced wicket to take Pakistan's total to 608 for seven before their skipper Intikhab called a halt. My return was nought for 102.

At Lord's it was a completely different story against virtually the same batting side. Of the nineteen Pakistan wickets that fell in that second Test of 1974 I had picked up thirteen at a total cost of 71 to make an England victory a pure formality until the rains returned on the final day to wash out the match.

The reason for my depression was the way my efforts had been dismissed, heavily criticized even, during the match at Edgbaston, and the matter-of-fact way my thirteen wickets had been accepted at Lord's. I don't think I was given the credit I deserved for either performance.

I certainly was not after the Edgbaston episode. I was dropped from the England side after that match and I doubt whether I would have played in another Test that summer if Norman Gifford, my replacement, had not broken a finger at Old Trafford.

This led to my recall for the final match that summer against India at the Oval.

My unrewarding stint in the Edgbaston Test in June, 1971, was really the start of the heavy criticism of my style of bowling on good wickets. There had been hints of criticism at various stages before that match, but during that game it became a flood. At the end of the first and second days as much space was used up in press reports about my bowling as there was to describe Zaheer's double century on his first Test appearance in this country, and the centuries by Asif and Mushtaq.

I can quote from one in particular: 'Underwood's method must have distressed the purists since he bowled to a semi-circular field of eight men more or less equidistant, theoretically saving one, with only a slip close in and he almost a supernumerary since the speed Underwood bowled at – much nearer medium than slow – was such that on so plumb a pitch the spin had no chance to bite.'

That was just a sample. The rest were slight variations on the same theme. I have already explained in the previous chapter my reasons for bowling to such a field. The calling on the part of the batsmen would have to be instant and correct if they wanted to push the ball towards a fielder and scamper for a single.

Not getting anything in the way of help from the wicket, I was making sure the batsmen earned every one of their runs. They were not going to take anything from me easily and cheaply. As for allowing the spin to bite, hardly anything deviated off the straight and narrow that day. There was no chance of turning the ball even a fraction, even though I used all the variations I possessed.

I think I succeeded in my main aim – that of keeping the batsmen in check, creating pressure for them and playing on their patience. My 18 overs on that first day cost only 39 runs, a rate of just over two runs an over. Zaheer, who had come in during the first over when Aftab Gull was taken off with a head wound when ducking into a bouncer from Alan Ward, spent the day making 159 runs. His century was not reached until just after tea. Mushtaq, his partner in their 291 stand, took almost six hours to reach three figures. Not exactly a hair-raising pace with Pakistan 300 on the board and only one wicket down.

Despite their slowness they played well, Zaheer in particular in the way he hit the ball through the offside with perfect timing and a generous pick-up. The wicket was just made for his method of batting, but it was not until Asif's entry on the afternoon of the second day that Pakistan made the progress expected of them in that situation. He provided the cream on top of the other innings, as he often does in that situation. Once he gets set he usually gathers momentum quickly and really takes some stopping.

At the end of it all I was naturally disappointed at not having taken a wicket, especially on the first day when I had kept Zaheer pinned down for some time, and struggling for a while. Yet I felt I had done as much as could have been expected of me in the conditions. I had been hit for 102 runs but I had bowled 41 overs. Nobody had got after me, which was pleasing in a total of more than 600.

I thought I had bowled well yet all the criticism from outside had obviously influenced the selectors, and I was put on the sidelines when the team was announced for the second Test against Pakistan at Lord's ten days later. Norman Gifford took my place and ran into the same criticism whenever he was asked to bowl on a good, flat wicket. Whenever I was supposed to have bowled badly there were calls for my head. Yet as soon as Gifford took over and failed to take a wicket there were calls for me to be reinstated – such is life at England level.

The Lord's Test against Pakistan in 1974 brought entirely different circumstances, but I felt upset afterwards because everybody seemed to accept that I was going to bowl them out. As if all I had to do was turn my arm over and the Pakistan batsmen would surrender. I did all that was expected of me. At the same time I had to earn those wickets.

It is not so easy to do, even on a wet wicket. It is easy for people to write, 'The wicket is just made for Underwood,' or 'Underwood should bowl them out today.' It is far harder waking up in the morning to read what people expect you to do and then go out and do it. I find there is enough tension playing in a Test match without extra pressure being put on me.

I could well understand the sympathy that was extended to the Pakistan players. What had been a good Lord's track became a difficult one after the torrential rain, but nobody was to blame for the covers being unable to stop all the water running down the Lord's slope and some getting on the wicket. Rain of that intensity comes only very rarely.

I can't deny the fact that I have enjoyed considerable success over the years on rain-affected wickets. Neither would I want to. But there is an art in bowling on such tracks. For me to be a real danger I have to get the ball to do something at the speed at which I bowl, or I have to find the most effective pace to use. There have been many occasions when I've bowled on a rain-affected wicket and the ball has done absolutely nothing.

That is why I feel so much extra pressure on me whenever rain does get on a wicket. If I don't take wickets in these circumstances then the public readily believe I have let England or Kent down. I am sure some of my England and Kent colleagues have felt I have let them down at times when the wicket has been wet and I have not managed to bowl the opposition out. It has become a standing joke in the England camp whenever rain is threatened. We can be out in the field when a dark cloud begins to form in the background and approach the ground. The other players will remark, 'That's a five for 40 cloud up there, Deadly.' I dread hearing that. The remark is passed as a joke but they must partly believe it themselves to have made it.

Believe me, that Lord's wicket for the Pakistan second innings in 1974 was not as difficult as their batsmen made it look. I suppose I gained some psychological advantage over them by taking five for 20 in their first innings total of 130 for nine declared, when they had also batted on a damp wicket. The majority of the batsmen surrendered more readily in their second innings than they should have done. I know I would have struggled to have bowled out most county sides at Lord's that day, and the majority of the Pakistan batsmen had gained sufficient experience of playing on wet wickets to have made more of a fight of it.

Mushtaq, for example, has the technique and the temperament to battle it out in those conditions but he seemingly made little attempt to get down to the pavilion end and take me. Most of his top score of 76 was made before the rain came, and I thought he let his side down that day. Obviously he didn't fancy me, and there was a reason for his anxiety. I have got Mushtaq out more times than any other batsman I've played regularly against.

I was pleased with my performance that Monday afternoon when play finally started, because I took my wickets from bowling over the wicket, something I had not done for several seasons. When I first started to bowl round the wicket, the ball did nothing and the pressure on me started to build even more.

I had been bowling over the wicket to the left-handed Wasim Raja, and when I noticed the ball turn a little I decided to stay that side of the wicket for the right-handers as well. The really damp patch was on a length on a line with the right-hander's leg stump. My line and length had to be just right to exploit it. The majority of the Pakistan batsmen were right-handers. Even using that damp patch the ball did not do very much. It stopped a little and turned a little, but not sufficiently for me to expect to beat the bat regularly. The only time I did in the entire innings was when Intikhab came in and tried to force it along by playing the occasional attacking shot with everybody up around the wicket. I took most of my wickets on that Monday through batsmen getting caught square and close in on either side of the wicket, with Greig at silly point and Lloyd at short square picking up the chances.

I felt afterwards that I had received very little credit for taking those eight wickets in the second innings. Simply because I had done exactly what people had expected me to do. No credit for being able to exploit the conditions with a measure of skill I had picked up over the years. The only comment I saw afterwards to that end came from another cricketer, Greig, writing in a national newspaper, when he said he doubted whether any other team would have been able to bowl Pakistan out in such a short time because they lacked a bowler with the ability. I was grateful for that.

Then again I should be grateful, I suppose, that I escaped lightly after what I consider my worst bowling in Tests. That was also in 1974, against India in the first match at Old Trafford. There was hardly a mention of it in the newspapers, yet I would not have had the slightest cause for complaint if the selectors had dropped me for the second Test. I was expecting it, and was greatly relieved when the axe did not fall.

The two players who were criticized were Greig and Denness. Greig was blamed for standing too close in at silly point where, it was argued, he was in no position to react quickly enough to accept the genuine nicks. Denness was criticized for not having a fielder on the wide third man or square cover boundary cutting off the runs. I was the cause, unwittingly, of much of the criticism.

On the question of Greig standing too close, he started to adopt that position on the tour to India where so many catches were taken close to the wicket. I like him up there when a new batsman has arrived at the crease. He is not there purely to take catches as so many people seem to think but, as has happened in the past, to force batsmen into error by his very presence. It undoubtedly has an unsettling effect on new arrivals, preventing them just pushing at the ball and waiting for one off the mark. They are forced to play a more positive shot which must increase the chance of a new arrival making an error.

That was exactly what Greig was doing at Old Trafford, particularly at the start of the partnership between Gavaskar and Viswanath in the India first innings when they added 73 for the fourth wicket, India's highest stand of the match.

All that happened was that these two used the avenue square of the wicket – to Greig's left hand – to find that square cover boundary several times, which resulted in the captain being criticized for not having a man out there. That was not Mike's fault but mine, because you cannot and must not set a field for a bad ball. That season I had been playing very little first class cricket until that Test. Most of the time had been spent playing in the Benson and Hedges Cup or the John Player League, in which I had been bowling a line of leg stump. At Old Trafford I found it difficult to suddenly switch back to my normal line of off stump for first class games, and as a result gave Gavaskar and Viswanath too much room in which to play the square cut. Being little in stature, they play that shot well. Fortunately the other England bowlers did well enough in both innings to cover my shortcomings.

Obviously nobody likes being criticized. I should have taken some hammer in that match but escaped. I took some in the Edgbaston match in 1971 which I felt wasn't justified. And twice I've come in for some criticism after bowling in Test matches at the Oval. On each occasion my critics were probably right.

In 1971 the first two Tests against India were drawn. The third one at the Oval resulted in India winning a Test match for the first time on English soil. It was also Ray Illingworth's first defeat by another country since taking over the England captaincy reins in 1969. In some quarters I was held partly responsible.

England had made a reasonable enough start in the Test match by scoring 355, which should have been enough to have put the question of defeat out of our minds. Nobody had scored a century but John Jameson, in his second Test match, had opened with a breezy 82 before being unluckily run out. Alan Knott and Dick Hutton had finally turned the match in England's favour with a 103 run seventh wicket partnership, Knotty being only 10 runs short of three figures when out to a return catch to Solkar.

It was a typical Oval wicket, getting slower and slower as each day passed, but there was just sufficient in it to help the spin bowler. Ray Illingworth took advantage of it to take five for 70 when India batted and were dismissed for 284, leaving England 71 runs ahead. Unfortunately I got very little out of the wicket and I failed to strike in India's first innings.

England's troubles – and mine to some extent – started on the Monday when we were bowled out for 101. Chandrasekhar was India's hero, his medium-paced leg-breaks claiming six for 38, but he was helped by some of the worst England batting I can remember. We should never have been dismissed for such a low score.

The fact that we were, the fact that Ray had taken five wickets in India's first innings and that another spinner, Chandra, had taken six in England's second innings, left many people believing England could win the match. India still had to make 173 for victory. It was left to Ray and me to stop them. Ray did his best but I wasn't able to offer him the support he needed at the other end.

Although I did not bowl as well as I could have done Ray still made it extremely tight, putting on the pressure as only he can, so that India lost six wickets before they got home. Much was expected of me because the wicket had lost all life by the last day and it was thought my extra pace might make the difference. I did take three wickets but gave away more runs than I should have done, those wickets costing 72 runs off my 38 overs.

The Indian batsmen, Wadekhar, Sardesai and Viswanath in particular, were able to take runs off me which they could not against Illingworth, who conceded only 40 runs off his 36 overs.

As well as taking some of the blame for that defeat I must also give credit to the Indian batsmen for the way they refused to be put off the victory trail.

Many other sides might well have cracked under the pressure, as Ray made sure nothing was given away in the field, but they grafted as I have never before seen Indian batsmen graft in inching their way along the path towards a historic victory. Viswanath, for instance, played three hours for his 33 and stayed until India were within three runs of victory before he was caught behind off the left-arm spin of Brian Luckhurst, Illingworth by then having conceded defeat.

Twelve months later, on the same ground, I know there was a feeling in some quarters that I might have done more to prevent Australia winning by five wickets, and so square the 1972 series two-all. The situations were very similar with Australia having to bat last, needing to score 241 to win on a dusting wicket.

That was a fascinating match from start to finish, swaying backwards and forwards from one side to the other. Australia were undoubtedly helped over the final leg by two tragic blows to England, when we lost both Ray Illingworth and John Snow, in addition to Basil d'Oliveira who had damaged a leg muscle in what was to be his final appearance for England. As in the match against India a year before, nobody made a century in England's first innings of 284. But once more Knott chipped in to rescue the side, this time making 92. What a comfort it has been to England over the years, knowing he has been available to bat number seven or eight.

Things started well for England on the second day when Australia's innings began. Graeme Watson, promoted to open the innings in an attempt to find a reliable partner for Keith Stackpole, was brilliantly caught down the leg side by Knott off Geoff Arnold, and then Snow removed the menace of Stackpole, bowling him with one that came in at him off the seam. Australia had lost both openers for 34, but then we were held up while history was made.

Greg Chappell came in to join his elder brother and captain Ian, and together they added 201 runs for the third wicket, both of them scoring centuries. By the time the Australian first innings had finished at 399, they had established a lead of 115. It was a handsome margin, but we were all encouraged by the sight of the ball stopping and turning just a little which enabled me to take four wickets for 90. The Australians still had to bat last on a wicket which was starting to dust.

To take advantage of any help from the wicket on the final day England needed a solid second innings score. Barry Wood, Lancashire's opening batsman, helped to provide it playing in his first Test match. Handling the menace of Dennis Lillee better than any other England batsman that summer, he scored 90 the second time round and England had made 356 when the second innings closed midway through the afternoon on the fourth day. Australia were left needing 242 runs to win with plenty of time to spare.

Before the day was out England were to suffer with Snow damaging a finger on his bowling hand, which limited his use, and Illingworth twisting his left ankle, pivoting on his follow through, which put him out of cricket for the rest of the season. John Edrich took over the captaincy and was left with only three fully fit regular bowlers when the last day started, Australia needing another 126 runs with eight second innings wickets left.

In the circumstances most people looked to me to stand between the Australians and the victory which would have allowed them to draw the series. After all, I was the one genuine and regular spin bowler left standing, the wicket was dusting and the odd ball misbehaved. As it turned out I could not prevent them winning, and I suppose that if I fail to bowl a side out on a wicket doing something then I haven't bowled as well as I should.

But it was expecting a lot of me, and I felt the pressure. I also missed Ray at the other end. Although Greig bowled well, taking two wickets for 31 in fifteen overs on that last day, it was not quite the same as having a spinner as partner. Fast bowlers always hunt better in pairs and spinners are more threatening when working as a team in conditions which assist them. Peter Parfit was given a go but he would be the first to admit that he did not bowl his off-spin regularly enough to be considered a match-winning force in those circumstances.

We were in with a chance when Greig had Keith Stackpole caught behind, and then was rewarded with a leg-before appeal against Ross Edwards. In between I had Ian Chappell caught and Australia lost three wickets for the addition of five runs, leaving them still 105 runs short of their target on 137 for four.

Only one more wicket was to fall however, that of Greg Chappell when I had him leg-before. The score was then 171 for five, another 71 wanted. Paul Sheahan and Rodney Marsh saw Australia home, Sheahan producing his best innings against England in making his undefeated 44.

Luck was not with us at all during that match. Before he had added to his overnight 70 Stackpole offered a sharp chance to slip off Arnold. In the first over I bowled to Greg Chappell one ball popped and just missed the edge of the bat. And when Australia were 178 for five Sheahan gave a very hard chance off me to Bob Willis, substituting for Illingworth, at short leg. Nobody could blame Bob for putting it down. Most fielders would have been taking cover but Bob stood his ground and Knott almost made the catch himself as the ball rebounded off Bob back towards the wicket.

I had not bowled badly against either India or Australia. Certainly that was true in the 1971 Test against India. As far as the match against Australia was concerned in 1972 the question of my pace was raised again. There was a feeling on the part of some critics that I had bowled a shade too fast to allow the ball an opportunity to bite on the dusting wicket. I have already expressed my feelings on that issue.

The Indians, of course, were over the moon following their first win on English soil at the Oval in 1971, but I don't think I have ever seen an opposing side so overcome with a victory than the Australians in 1972. They felt justice had been done after their defeat in three days in the previous match at Headingley. They had left Yorkshire complaining bitterly they had been cheated by the wicket.

I was brought in for my first Test of the summer, replacing Norman Gifford who had played in the first three. The pitch was damp and slow, taking spin on the first day. The suspicious Australians were putting two and two together and making five. Several claimed it was a deep-laid plot designed to help me and reduce the pace of Dennis Lillee to little more than medium fast. By the Saturday evening they were making two and two add up to six, seven and eight after being bowled out for 146 and 136, leaving us winners by nine wickets and two–one ahead in the series.

It wasn't a good Test wicket by any means, but there had been no skulduggery. The whole ground had been flooded the weekend before the Test by violent storms, and the wicket had been attacked by a fungus called fusarium which damages the grass. The Australians contributed towards their own downfall by some poor batting, and had also left out Johnny Gleeson, reducing their attack to one recognized spinner. It was just pure coincidence that I happened to be recalled for that match. In the three previous Tests Gifford had taken only one wicket. He was most unlucky. In those three Tests the conditions had not helped him and he had bowled only 34 overs. He was dropped, I took over and found the conditions so helpful I bowled 31 overs in the Australian first innings.

That, as they say, is how the cookie crumbles. In the previous Test match on a good, flat Trent Bridge wicket Gifford had been the subject of the same complaints with regard to the pace of his bowling and flattish trajectory as I had received. He had paid the price for not satisfying the purists as I had done at Edgbaston 14 months before.

I enjoyed bowling in that Headingley match. Before lunch Ray Illingworth and I were in harness and operating as a team. Between us we bowled 52 overs of the 87 Australia used up making their first innings 146, and managed to work perfectly together. After a shaky start, when I was hit for 10 runs off my first two overs, I settled into my rhythm, keeping it tight, and Ray bowled immaculately from the other end. We had to work hard to get something out of the wicket because it was so slow, but the damp helped. If the Australians had been prepared to work at their batting in the way John Inverarity did in their first innings, they could have made nearer 200.

Of the first seven Australian batsmen Keith Stackpole was the only one to succeed with 52, his fifth score of 50 or more in the series. He had lost Edwards, bowled for a duck by Snow, with the score at 10, but a reasonable Australian total still seemed possible as Ian Chappell joined Stackpole in taking it up to 79. Then their troubles began. They lost their next six wickets for the addition of only 19 runs, which left them tottering on 98 for seven before Inverarity and Mallett joined together to add a touch of respectability to the final score.

Alan Knott started it when he held a catch behind off Stackpole against me, and I followed by getting Greg Chappell leg-before.

Illingworth then had a hand in the next four wickets. He took a return catch to dismiss Ian Chappell and bowled Doug Walters before taking catches at silly point against Sheahan and Marsh off my bowling.

That was the extent of our wicket taking in the first innings. With fingers aching we gave way to the new ball after Inverarity and Mallett had put on 47. Both are tall men who use their feet and reach well to smother the danger from the spin, but the new ball removed the tail.

Disappointed as the Australians must have been with their total they began to look far happier on the second day. We lost seven wickets for 128, John Edrich having scored 45, and Tony Greig 24, but nobody else reaching 20. Illingworth made sure the advantage was not surrendered, battling through three hours for his 57 and helped by Snow making 48. They added 104 for the eighth wicket, a partnership which was to make sure of victory. Without Gleeson, off spinner Mallett had to work overtime, and bowled 52 overs in taking his five for 114. He was helped by Inverarity, who found himself pressed into Test match service as a left-arm spinner.

In the end we managed a 117 run first innings lead, which was almost enough for victory with the Australians collapsing a second time. They lost nine wickets for 111, and only a last wicket partnership between Sheahan and Massie saved them from an innings defeat.

The breakthrough was provided by Geoff Arnold this time in removing Edwards – who collected a pair – and Ian Chappell for ducks, both caught behind the wicket. The Australians never recovered. Before the shine had been removed Illingworth had sent me into battle and I managed to take the next five wickets as they stumbled along to 69 for seven. Sheahan, batting with great concentration and fine technique, and Mallett held us up briefly before Illingworth bowled the latter. I nipped in for Lillee's wicket and Illingworth finally dismissed Massie leaving England needing only 19 to win. And win we did with ninety minutes to spare on the third day.

That was one of the most important matches of my Test career, my ten wickets in the game among the most treasured I have taken. I had appeared in only one of England's previous eight Test matches and then only as a result of an injury to

Gifford. From Edgbaston in June 1971 to Headingley in July 1972 Gifford had been getting the vote over me whenever the England selectors had met.

If they had backed him one more time and played him at Headingley there is no doubt that, on the Headingley wicket as it was for the Australian game, he would have picked up wickets cheaply as well. He would have stayed for the next match and today I might still be on the outside as far as Test cricket is concerned. That is why I shall always remember Headingley, 1972.

5. TRIUMPHS AND DISAPPOINTMENTS

Against the Australians, 1968 . . . New Zealand, and my Test best . . . Five wickets, a 'radio job' performance . . . disappointment in the West Indies.

The Oval is far from being one of my favourite Test centres. It is certainly the most depressing, in my opinion, of the six Test grounds used in England and most of those overseas. I find it cold, drab, unfriendly and lacking in atmosphere, which is not altogether surprising since I was nursed on the tree-lined, tent-ringed fields of Canterbury, Maidstone, Tunbridge Wells and the like.

Surrey's headquarters has not been one of my luckiest grounds either in recent years, yet it provided the setting for two of my outstanding memories of Test cricket.

I doubt whether anything will compare with that fantastic victory against the Australians at the Oval in 1968 which enabled England to draw the series one-all. A series in which England had been the better side after the first Test defeat at Old Trafford, but had been prevented by the weather from having a chance to prove it in terms of results. And once again it looked as though the weather was going to have the last word on the final day of the Oval Test when the heavens opened, turning the playing area into a large lake with isolated patches of green sticking through here and there.

There was never any question of Australia winning the match on that final day. They were 86 for five, still 265 behind when the rain started during the lunch interval. By the time the ground was fit to play again after scores of spectators had become volunteer groundsmen for the afternoon, only 78 minutes remained in which to take the last five Australian wickets.

An impossible task. At least I thought so. So did most of the other members of the side. Our fears seemed confirmed when absolutely nothing happened for the first 42 minutes after play resumed on the final evening. But there was one man who always thought it was on, and he was the man who mattered: the skipper, Colin Cowdrey. His enthusiasm and blind conviction that England could do it kept us going during those 42 minutes when Inverarity and wicketkeeper Barry Jarman were steadily playing out time. Colin was proved right with just six minutes to spare.

That summer we had been beaten by 159 runs in the opening Test of the series in Manchester. Rain had prevented certain England victories in the second and third Tests at Lord's and Edgbaston respectively, and the sides had emerged from the fourth Test at Headingley with another draw in a match that had been even throughout.

Instead of being one down in the series, England should have entered the final Test with a 2–1 advantage. I think that was the reason why Colin was so determined to win the match on the final day. Until that rain everything had gone according to Colin's planning, including winning the toss.

Before the match England had made one dramatic decision which was to prove a vital factor in the game itself, as well as to change the whole structure of world cricket. Two days before the start Roger Prideaux, the former Kent batsman who was then playing for Northants, was forced to pull out of the team with a heavy cold. He had made a most impressive debut in the previous game against Australia at Headingley.

In his place Basil d'Oliveira was selected. The Cape Coloured all-rounder had not played for England since the first Test that summer, and had not been in particularly good form for Worcestershire. Colin felt that d'Oliveira's inclusion was necessary to field a balanced England side, and ignored the fact that England were due to visit South Africa that winter. The selectors gave Colin their complete backing.

D'Oliveira took his chance magnificently when the time came on the first evening. A dogged 130 not out by John Edrich on the first day, plus a sparkling 63 from Tom Graveney, had helped England to 238 for four when d'Oliveira made his entry. That evening he started by straight driving the off-spin of Mallett –

playing in his first Test – for six and carried on in the same vein the following day.

Dolly was so confident that on the first evening he telephoned his wife Naomi and his two sons at home and told them to 'just watch that Test match on television tomorrow'. Edrich added another 34 runs, but Dolly dominated the second day with an innings of 158 before England were all out for 494 runs. Just the type of score Colin was hoping for in his search for revenge.

With no chance of winning, Australia's one plan was to drag their first innings out for as long as possible. In a mission such as this they had the greatest of experts in their captain Bill Lawry. After one long, almost strokeless innings he had been described by one cricket writer as 'a corpse with pads on'. In this Test he resembled a still life picture even more. He began his innings on the second evening and was still at the crease when the fourth morning started with only 135 runs against his name.

He did not score another run but his ending was controversial when given out caught behind against Snow. Lawry claimed he played outside the ball which then went between his arm and body.

With only Gleeson and Connolly to come the Australian first innings ended 170 runs behind. We quickly built that advantage to 351 by sacrificing wickets for runs the second time round, and left the Australians to cope with the final thirty-five minutes that night when they began their second innings.

We expected Lawry to be the main stumbling block. There is nothing he likes more than to occupy the crease in a lost cause position, but he was out again that night, and there was no doubt about it this time, being taken off bat and pad by Milburn at short leg against the bowling of Brown. There were three overs each from our opening bowlers before Colin gave me a chance and in my second over, the last of the day, I had Redpath leg-before when he padded up to a ball which straightened. Australia finished that fourth evening on 13 for two, with six hours remaining to negotiate for their last eight wickets.

Slowly we chipped away at the Australian innings on that last morning, the sky blue for the most part, and with no sign of any rain to threaten our hopes. Illingworth and I shared the attack for most of that two and a half hour pre-lunch session, with occasional bursts from Snow and Brown. I won another leg-before appeal, this time against Ian Chappell, and saw Doug Walters caught behind, beaten by the turn, while Illingworth nipped in to have Paul Sheahan caught just before lunch. Playing with great care and attention to detail, Inverarity was solidly holding up one end but the odds were still heavily in our favour at the break, when Australia had scored 86 for five. Jarman was in with Inverarity, but there was little batting to come.

Somebody has since told me that the first drops of rain fell at exactly 1.27. Within ten minutes the rain was torrential. After half an hour most of the grass had disappeared under an inch of water. Another thirty minutes and the sun was shining brilliantly, but there seemed no chance of the match starting again. I remember gazing down at the scene from the England dressing-room and thinking to myself, 'That's it. We'll never get out there again.' Like the others, I began to pack my cricket bag.

I can still picture now the sight of Colin going out to the middle, his trousers pulled high over his boots, urging the Oval groundstaff in their work. Soon the outfield was dotted with volunteers mopping up the water following a loudspeaker appeal. Gradually the water drained away, the patches of green began to grow larger and link up again. The large hand on the Vauxhall Lane stand clock showed just past twenty to five when Snow went off on his run once more.

Nothing happened. The wicket itself was still saturated, but for forty minutes Colin switched from one bowler to another, seeking to lure Inverarity and Jarman into error. Finally d'Oliveira made the breakthrough. The ball was just short of a length, short enough for Jarman to believe he could safely leave it alone. He raised his bat shoulder high, only for the ball to clip the top of the off stump. Only thirty-six minutes were left, another four wickets were wanted. It still seemed impossible.

Immediately he had taken the wicket d'Oliveira was whipped off and I replaced him at the pavilion end to take on Mallett, the new batsman. I must admit the pressure got to me that day. Although the wicket was drying it was still not doing anything, and in my frustration I just bowled faster and faster. Umpire Charlie Elliott told me afterwards that I was a genuine medium pace at the end.

By now all the fielders were clustered around the bat. They were dominated by the 6ft 5in frame of David Brown at forward short leg lunging forward every time a batsman played a forward defensive stroke and picking up the ball off the middle of the wicket.

D'Oliveira was at backward short leg, Milburn at short square leg. Then came Brown with Snow at silly mid-on. Directing operations was Colin at first slip with Graveney next to him. Illingworth was in the gully, Edrich at silly point and Dexter at silly mid-off, with Knott the wicket-keeper completing the ring. They all seemed to be in touching distance of each other and the batsman.

Twice in one over Brown swooped forward to scoop up catches inches from the ground to dismiss two batsmen and give me two wickets. Both Mallett and McKenzie had lunged forward to smother the ball but had not quite managed to get over it.

That made it 110 for eight with 27 minutes left when Gleeson came in. While Inverarity did his best to take the bowling, Gleeson attempted to scatter the ring of close-in fielders. Several times he hit out boldly but only once did he connect, sweeping me for four. For 13 minutes he held out but then I bowled him with a ball that did nothing. It pitched outside the off stump and carried on to hit middle and off. Nine wickets down and 13 minutes to go.

It was down to six minutes when I took the last wicket. Not that of last man Connolly but Inverarity, who had opened the innings with Lawry the previous evening and had stood defiant throughout. Finally the pressure told on him too. He misjudged the ball that went with my arm, was rapped on the pads, and up went Elliott's finger to end his gallant stand and give England the victory. He may not look a leg-before victim on the picture which is most commonly used to show that last dramatic moment, but he was plumb in front.

The last four Australian wickets had fallen to me for six runs in twenty-seven deliveries, giving me innings figures of seven for 50. Those last 78 minutes seemed like a lifetime. I was shattered at the end of it, and felt no particular joy or elation at the time. My first desire was to get back to the dressing-room, and I remember thinking to myself how peaceful it looked as I entered the deserted room. It did not stay empty for long.

I was just twenty-three and playing in only my eighth Test match. The occasion was almost too much for me. When I finally broke free of the celebrations and the crowded pavilion I met my parents, brother and his fiancée outside the Oval. My mother, in particular, was very emotional, almost in tears. They naturally wanted to rush home and see it all on television, but all I wanted was to get away from the whole atmosphere and have a quiet meal. I had my wish and we ended up at a steak bar in Bromley before returning to my parents' home, where the phone did not stop ringing until the middle of the night.

I never did see the action replay on television that night. Since then I have seen the odd clip showing one or two wickets falling, but I have never seen the whole of that last seventy-eight minutes replayed. I would like to see it again, relive the whole dramatic period from start to finish. At the time of writing it is my outstanding memory of my cricket career.

Looking back I suppose that performance led to me being tagged as a 'wet wicket demon' although I was given full credit for my bowling at the time. I was, too, the following summer in the three match series against New Zealand when I picked up twenty-four wickets – eleven in the first match at Lord's, one in the drawn second Test at Trent Bridge and twelve in the final match at the Oval.

The Lord's Test was a severe set-back for the New Zealand captain Graham Dowling. The team had arrived in this country while England were engaged in a three match series against the West Indies, and had been criticized for slow scoring. Dowling announced that his side would play positive attacking cricket even if England would not – and then watched his side dismissed for 169 and 131 in the opening Test, losing by 230 runs.

To be fair to Dowling and explain my own bowling return, that Lord's wicket was not up to Test standard. Just like that Headingley wicket against the Australians in 1972, the Lord's square was having trouble with the fusarium at the time, and the bounce was unpredictable like so many county wickets today. Forty wickets fell during the match but only two players managed to get past 50. Illingworth did so in England's first innings of 190, and Edrich mastered the conditions superbly in England's second innings of 340 when he made 115.

That match marked the Test debut of Derbyshire's Alan Ward who had not had even one championship match to his credit 12 months before. He made a far happier debut than I did, taking a wicket in his third over when Glenn Turner was caught behind as New Zealand set out to match our 190.

It looked well within their capabilities as Dowling was joined by Congdon. Together they took the score to 76 before Illingworth, at silly point, took a catch off his rival captain to give me my first wicket. From then on New Zealand struggled, wickets falling regularly to Illingworth and myself. I finished the innings with four for 38, Illingworth slightly better at four for 37.

The real drama as far as I was concerned started on the fourth day when England's second innings had come to an end, leaving New Zealand with the task of 362 to win or almost eleven hours to survive to obtain a draw. Neither looked possible and our victory seemed only a matter of time, unless rain stepped in.

Ward provided the early breakthrough again, this time having Dowling taken behind. The New Zealanders had needed a long innings from him to give them confidence, but he was back in the pavilion with only five runs on the board. That must have knocked a lot of heart out of their batting. Turner apart, there was no sign of any real resistance until the tail-enders came in.

Like the Pakistan batsmen at Lord's in 1974 I believe the New Zealand batsmen allowed the wicket to upset them more than it should have. Looking at its bare patches, with odd bits of green in between, they conditioned themselves into thinking the fight was lost. In truth I doubt whether the wicket was doing any more on that fourth afternoon than it had done on the first. The bounce was unpredictable, and the wicket two-paced, but it was not that difficult for a batsman intent on survival, as Turner showed.

He remained undefeated, the sixteenth batsman to carry his bat in Test cricket and, at twenty-two, the youngest. He has, of course, a wonderful Barrington-like temperament and a very sound technique. He also possesses a wider range of strokes than he often shows, as he demonstrated in 1973 when he became the first player since 1938 to score 1000 runs before the end of May.

Turner apart, the rest folded weakly. They made no real attempt to score off me as I took the next seven wickets to fall. At one stage I had five for five. That became six for 12 and then seven for 18. Only then did I come across a batsman who was prepared to have a go. My seven for 18 became seven for 32 when Dayle Hadlee three times drove me back over my head for four.

That was too much for Illingworth who immediately took me off and turned to the pace of Ward to blast out the tail. That was a great disappointment. I didn't think too much of my captain at that moment. When you have got seven and only a couple of tail-enders to come you immediately think of eight or nine wickets. Yet looking at it dispassionately Illingworth was right. I had bowled 31 overs at that stage, my fingers, arms and legs were aching, and my bowling had lost its edge. I'd given the game away by bowling a no ball which started that little spree by Hadlee. So seven for 32 off 31 overs was my limit, a Test best performance at that stage of my life.

The batsmen were certainly not beaten by any turn or lift. As Illingworth said afterwards, 'The wicket was never a real turner.' I took the majority of the wickets with the ball that went with my arm, the batsmen playing for the turn and playing outside it. I had two leg-befores and two clean-bowleds with that ball.

My twelve wickets against New Zealand at the Oval were much harder to come by, especially the six in the second innings on a wicket described by cricket writers as 'blameless'.

The first innings had been different. The New Zealanders – quite properly – had decided to bat first on winning the toss, but then their luck deserted them when the day was interrupted by two or three showers. It was after the first long shower had livened up the wicket that I was able to get to work. Until the rain Congdon and Turner had been batting well, particularly in the spell immediately after lunch. The rain halted them for forty-five minutes and I was able to strike just after tea when the wicket was drying. In seventeen overs I was rewarded with four wickets at a cost of 17 runs – Turner and Congdon among them – and added two more the next morning to give me my first innings six for 41. They were all out for 150, a total we passed for the loss of just four wickets on our way to a first innings lead of 92. But the going was sticky in the face of some tight left-arm spin bowling from Hedley Howarth.

He conceded only 66 runs off his thirty-four overs and deserved more than his two wickets. As a member of the same union I felt sorry for him, and he would surely have earned his just reward if he had Illingworth setting the field for him. As a result of his accuracy we took ninety-eight overs to score those 242 first innings runs. The scoring rate would have been slower still but for Ward smashing Taylor for 18 in one over, four times reaching the boundary. Not that Ward had much idea where the ball was going, as he admitted afterwards.

By the time New Zealand started their second innings there was little wrong with the wicket. It had dried completely and we knew we would be faced with a wearing-down, whittling-out exercise for the rest of the match. In fact it took 106 overs to end their innings for 229, leaving us to get 138 to win.

They were in no hurry. They had nowhere to go but stuck to their journey with solid determination, especially Hastings who scored highest with 61. Illingworth was not helped in his task by losing Arnold with a bruised heel. He was forced to juggle the rest of us around in bursts, trying to upset the batsmen by posing them new problems as frequently as he could. I got another six but there was nothing dramatic about my performance.

They were earned by bowling a line and length, putting the batsmen under pressure by restricting their run scoring until they eventually lost patience. This is my policy on a good wicket and it worked.

Over the years the New Zealand batsmen have provided me with a healthy proportion of my Test match wickets. On figures alone those performances at Lord's and the Oval should rank high among my achievements at a Test level. So should my twelve for 97 against them at Christchurch in March 1971. Yet the one I pride myself on more than any other was my five for 108 return at Auckland later that month.

Why? Simply because that wicket was a beauty. And after Australia and all the criticism at home about my lack of penetration on good wicket conditions I think it was essential at that stage of my life to convince myself I had the ability to bowl sides out when the wicket was doing nothing to help me.

I am happy in my own mind that I did not let England down on the tour of Australia. I finished with sixteen wickets in the series – second to Snow – as well as doing the job Illingworth mapped out for me: that of keeping the batsmen in check while Snow, Lever and Willis were being rested. My one disappointment was not being able to pick up five wickets in any of the Australian innings.

Perhaps I'm too figure-conscious, but taking five wickets is important to me. It seems to have become the standard figure indicating a good performance from an ordinary one, yet one wicket in an innings can be a match-winning performance – if it's the wicket that ends a threatening partnership, for instance.

Record books list performances of five wickets in an innings, ten wickets in a match. 'That's a radio job' is a saying amongst the lads in cricket whenever a bowler takes his fifth wicket. For whenever scores are given on the radio a mention is always made of a five wicket performance. A bowler may take four for 25 and his name is missed out. Yet one who takes five for 100 is named. So often that fifth wicket proves elusive.

That day in Auckland, the fifth wicket did not get away and I succeeded in completing my 'radio job'. The other four I had taken the previous day when New Zealand started their first innings in answer to our 317. In six and a quarter hours' batting they managed only 208 runs, losing four batsmen on a wicket full of runs and a fast outfield.

I felt shattered by the end of that day, having bowled the equivalent of thirty-six six-ball overs, but I was extremely happy in the way I had taken the wickets through subtle variations of pace, my only real weapon in the conditions. The first break was a long time coming with openers Turner and Dowling spending almost three hours over their partnership of 96. Then I deceived Dowling with my slower ball which he failed to spot, drove too early and gave me a return catch.

Four balls later, before the new batsman Congdon had settled down, I bowled him with a fast yorker and later induced both Turner and Morgan into giving me return catches. Like Dowling, they both failed to read my slower delivery and did not get on top of the ball as they attempted to drive. I might have had another one that evening because I thought I found the glove of Shrimpton with Knott taking the catch behind. The umpire turned down the appeal but Illingworth, fielding at gully and perfectly placed to see everything, remained convinced Shrimpton had gloved the ball.

It was Shrimpton who provided me with my fifth wicket – my hundredth in Test cricket – the following day after a long wait. He was six when I thought I had him caught on that second evening and 46 when I was rewarded with a leg-before shout against him. On that previous evening his partner Burgess had almost given a catch to Edrich off me, the ball dropping just short. He stayed to make 104, New Zealand finally declaring eight runs behind on 317 for seven.

In all it was a strange match, with New Zealand threatening by the end of the third day to beat England for the first time in Tests. It was our final match of the Australia–New Zealand tour and we were all desperately tired after more than five months away from home, which partly explained our poor batting on the first and third days. Poor, that is, with the exception of Knott.

He had saved us in the first innings when he made his debut among Test century-makers after we had lost six wickets for 145. More than 100 of those runs had come from Cowdrey and d'Oliveira, who each made half centuries. In making his gallant stand Knotty found an ideal partner in Lever. Together they added 149 for the seventh wicket and Knott's second 50 took only 48 minutes. He had just reached his 'ton' when he was bowled playing back against Collinge and the new ball. Thanks to these two we reached 321.

We did not bat any better the second time round and were in great danger of defeat. When our second innings started Cowdrey was back at the hotel nursing a hamstring injury and a heavy cold. By then Illingworth had already announced that d'Oliveira would bat again only in a dire emergency, since he had torn a calf muscle and was hardly able to walk. An S.O.S. message was soon on its way to Cowdrey to report to the ground as we lost wickets quickly.

Four had gone down for 67 before Cowdrey came in, and together with Knott helped to pull us round. Finally, Cowdrey, with Luckhurst running for him, just failed to make his second half century of the match. Knott stayed longer and looked set to become the first English batsman to score a century in each innings of a Test match since Denis Compton against Australia at Adelaide in 1947. He needed only four more when he was bowled by Cunis.

We were still not out of trouble. The crisis was sufficient for d'Oliveira to hobble to the wicket, Hampshire running for him, and stay fifty minutes over his five runs. The five runs were not important but the fifty minutes made sure New Zealand did not have sufficient time to knock off the 246 runs they eventually needed for victory. They had only two hours left by the time our rearguard action had come to an end.

Just before that second and final Test in Auckland the New Zealand Cricket Council kindly presented me with the ball with which I had taken my 1000th wicket in first class cricket a few days before. That was during the first Test in Christchurch when I took twelve wickets in the game.

On that occasion I couldn't really have asked for any more help from the wicket. It was damp and soft with a few thin strips of grass and cracks on the surface before the match started. It was made worse during the lunch interval when a thunderstorm gave it a thorough drenching. By then New Zealand had already lost four wickets for 33, three of them falling to Shuttleworth. Somehow he managed to get a little bounce from the wicket and both Murray and Morgan were out caught hooking.

I had managed just one wicket before lunch, but it was after the break that the conditions really suited me. I felt a little sympathy for Dowling who had fought manfully to survive during the two hours before lunch, making only 13 runs. Then he got a really nasty one the third ball after the wicket had dried from the thunderstorm. It stopped, turned, and lifted and he had no chance of getting his bat out of the way. When Glenn Turner, batting at number six in an attempt to provide the New Zealand middle order with a little solidity, was bowled as he went for the strike, the end was in sight and New Zealand were bowled out for 65.

Although over their years in county cricket our batsmen have learned the right technique to apply to these conditions, it was still tough going when we batted. We were 95 for four at one stage before d'Oliveira scored exactly 100, a masterly performance. He enabled us to take a 166 run lead on first innings. It was not sufficient to take us to an innings victory. The wicket had obviously improved by the time New Zealand batted a second time although Glenn Turner (76), Congdon (55) and Pollard (34) still needed to show a high degree of skill and technique in taking New Zealand's second innings to 254. This time my six wickets cost me 85 runs. We won the match by eight wickets.

Those seventeen wickets in the two matches against New Zealand at the end of the 1970–71 Australian tour, and the twenty four in three matches against them in England in 1969, contrast sharply with my returns against the West Indies. Since making my debut against them at Trent Bridge in 1966 I've played eleven Tests against them and taken 20 wickets.

In four Tests against the West Indies on the 1974 tour to the Caribbean I managed only five wickets – figures that still compare favourably with the other England bowlers on the tour apart from Greig. Switching to his slower style and using his height to obtain a degree of bounce nobody else could find, he was the only England bowler to reach double figures for wickets in the series, finishing with a total of 24, a marvellous performance.

One of the reasons given for my low striking rate against the West Indies over the years is the number of left-handed batsmen they have had in their sides, particularly today. On the last tour four of their first six batsmen were left-handers – Fredericks, Kallicharran, Lloyd and Sobers. Bowling to left-handers has proved to be my weakness in terms of figures.

This theory developed about two years ago when one cricket writer made a study of my Test match victims and discovered I numbered very few left-handed batsmen among them. And I am sure it was true at one stage of my career that I found bowling to left-handers far more difficult than to right-handers. I've also an explanation. In my early years with Kent I was given little experience against them.

The ball moving away from the batsman is always the more difficult to counter. Being a left-arm spinner, the majority of my deliveries are aimed at turning the ball away from the right-handed batsman – the same as a leg spinner. The bowler who turns the ball away from a left-handed batsman is the off spinner. Colin Cowdrey adopted that theory – with great success – during my early years with Kent. If I was bowling on a wicket helping the spinners when a left-handed batsman came in, Colin usually put Alan Dixon on to bowl his off-spinners. The result was that my experience against them was somewhat limited until my Test career started. My recent experience in the West Indies of bowling to them regularly on good wickets has now helped me to find the right line against them and my confidence has now been boosted accordingly.

All this doesn't explain my lack of success against them in 1966. They had few left-handers then and my first two Tests – the only two I played that summer – ended with me taking only one wicket.

I did not take a wicket at all on my Test debut. I had been

brought into the side after the West Indies had won the first Test at Old Trafford on a spinner's wicket, a defeat which cost Mike Smith the captaincy although he had been regarded almost as a hero only six weeks before when drawing the 1965–66 series in Australia one-all. Colin Cowdrey had taken over for the second Test at Lord's, which was drawn when Sobers and his cousin David Holford rescued the West Indies with a record-breaking unbeaten sixth wicket partnership of 274 in the second innings. They were only nine runs ahead and had lost five second innings wickets when the pair teamed up.

Back in 1963 I had taken five for 66 against the West Indies when playing for Kent, and maybe this helped sway the selectors. I was brought in for left-arm fast bowler Jeff Jones, and Illingworth was brought in for Titmus. There is that Illingworth-Underwood link again. Not that we had much opportunity to operate as a spinning team in the West Indies first innings. As usual at Trent Bridge there was a little in the wicket on the first morning for the faster bowlers, and Snow and Higgs used it well in taking four wickets each. I was given only two overs. To make matters worse I dropped a skier from Peter Lashley off Basil d'Oliveira and spent the next hour praying another catch wouldn't come my way. I should have caught it on the long leg boundary. Another chance did come my way, this time of Kanhai when he was driving at Higgs. I managed to hang on to it and so played my part in claiming a wicket in Tests for the first time.

I had plenty of opportunity during the second innings to take my first Test wicket as the West Indies went on a go-slow to ensure victory with a substantial lead. The West Indies had been all out for 235 in their first innings, giving us a 90-run advantage, and Sobers and company were not taking any chances the second time round with two and a half days still to go. By the time they declared with five wickets down they had made 482.

After just two overs in the first innings I was given 43 in the second. There wasn't much chance of a wicket with Butcher in such splendid form, and he went on to make an unbeaten 209. I didn't get many past the bat and all I could do was to bowl as economically as possible. By the time the innings had finished I had conceded exactly two runs an over, which was not too bad in an innings of that size.

In the next Test at Headingley, the West Indies won by an

innings and 55 runs to follow their 139-run win at Trent Bridge. But I did manage to get one wicket this time, that of Kanhai who was caught at mid-off by Graveney. My slower ball had worked again. It cost me 81 runs off 24 overs with Sobers and Nurse going on a run spree on the second day. Both scored centuries and added 265 runs for the fifth wicket in four hours.

That innings defeat cost Cowdrey the England leadership for the final Test against the West Indies at the Oval. It also cost me my England place. In the team shake-up that followed Brian Close's first appointment as England captain, I was dropped. I had no cause for complaint, especially with Close leading England to a thrilling victory.

The visit of the West Indies to England that summer caused many shake-ups in the England side. Only one player kept his place throughout the summer and played in all five Test matches. That was Ken Higgs, then of Lancashire and now with Leicestershire. Astonishing really, especially when one compares it with the policy of the England selectors today who try to keep the same team together and limit changes to the minimum. I think the present course is the right one.

6. GREAT BATSMEN, GREAT CRICKETERS

D'Oliveira, my 'Mr Cricket' . . . Sobers, the cricketer and the man . . . Great innings on bad wickets . . . Dexter storms back . . . A look at the world's great batsmen.

Basil d'Oliveira is my 'Mr Cricket'. What a marvellous character he is. When I write that he is my 'Mr Cricket' I'm not discussing him as a batsman, bowler or fielder. In each category he would be down the list somewhat when placing in order the best I have seen. It was d'Oliveira's whole approach and attitude which got through to me.

As a bowler I shall remember him in Test matches as a breaker up of dangerous partnerships. He wasn't a great wicket-taker, more a stock bowler. Yet whenever a partnership began to reach menacing proportions and all the other bowlers had failed to end it, up would come Dolly to try his hand. It is remarkable the number of times he succeeded.

As a fielder he often went into the slips at the beginning of his England career but gradually became – like me – a long leg and mid-off specialist. Even when the years began to catch up with him and he was not quite so fast off the mark or speedy across the ground as in his earlier days, no batsman could ever take advantage. There was never a question of 'one for the throw' when he had the ball in his hands. He had a remarkable 'arm' and could return the ball over the top of the wicket at either end no matter where he was positioned.

Yet it was as a batsman that he really impressed me. All seemed to be peace and calm with him, whatever the depth of the crisis England were in. He was never worried or hurried. The situation could be really desperate but he would still walk to the wicket as if he were out on a Sunday afternoon stroll. Once he arrived at the wicket he would stand there looking completely in charge of the situation, a rather arrogant, even disdainful look about him as he faced up to the bowlers.

If he felt any pressure he never showed it. He never accepted the word defeat until the match was actually lost. Whatever the strength and the reputation of the opposition, Dolly always considered England the better side. He was a wonderful influence in the dressing-room.

He scored five centuries for England in his forty-four Test matches, but those figures do not do justice to the value of his performances. I'm sure he would have scored more if he had batted just a little higher. Most of those five were scored batting six or seven, which meant he usually had tail-enders as partners for most of his time in the crease. The runs he did score for England were a tribute to his ability to farm the bowling.

Although I did not take any wickets on my Test debut, and collected only one catch in addition to putting one down, I did manage to get my name in the record books for a very short while – thanks to Dolly. Together we established a new last wicket record partnership for England against the West Indies of 65. Shared is rather an ambitious word on my part for my contribution was 12! The record stood for less than six weeks, being shattered completely during the final Test at the Oval that summer when Snow and Higgs put on 128 for the final wicket.

The way I felt when I walked to the wicket one ball would have been enough to have accounted for me. I had still not got over the fact that I was actually playing in a Test and sharing a dressing-room with such schoolboy heroes as Tom Graveney, Colin Cowdrey, Jim Parks, etc. Graveney had been recalled to the England side that summer after an absence of four years, and he responded with a typical Graveney century at Trent Bridge, crammed with flowing front foot cover drives piercing the field when and how he chose. Cowdrey, too, had played a brilliant innings of 96, but England were still only 25 runs ahead of West Indies' first innings of 235 when I entered the battlefield at the fall of the ninth wicket.

Dolly was then on 25 and must have been almost as nervous at the start of his innings as I felt. He was playing in only his second Test and the West Indies attack, spearheaded by Hall and Griffiths and supported by Sobers and Gibbs, was striving hard to limit England's first innings lead. Yet Dolly made everything appear so calm it was like a yachtsman being caught on a millpond when he had put to sea in a force eight gale. Dolly handled the bowling so skilfully that I was apparently at the wicket for an hour before I faced the first ball of an over.

He just picked his ones when he wanted, however Sobers set the field, and built up my confidence by quiet words of encouragement. I had not been at the wicket long when he strolled down between an over and said: 'How are you doing down your end, Blunders?' He was the only person to call me by that name.

I told him, 'I don't fancy facing Lance Gibbs much.'

He just nodded, strolled back down the other end and I hardly faced Gibbs again in the partnership. While I scored 12, Dolly took his score to 76 before he was bowled by Hall off an inside edge when driving.

I consider myself fortunate to have been his partner for a while during two of his finest centuries for England, and became completely absorbed watching another three figure innings. My first was only a brief stay with him while he put the finishing touches to his 158 against the Australians at the Oval in 1968. He was out while I was at the wicket. The second time was much longer when he saved England with a century on a very dodgy wicket in Dacca, East Pakistan, about six months later.

The wicket was a dusty, slow turner, and the situation was already tense when the match started because students controlled the town after days of rioting and bloodshed, during which the Army and the police had decided to withdraw to the outskirts of East Pakistan's capital. Les Ames, the tour manager, was supposed to have been warned of the situation before we had flown in, but the message was lost along the diplomatic channels. When we discovered there would be no police on duty inside or outside the ground we were all for going back to West Pakistan, until the student leaders warned us: 'Your coach would never make the airport.'

It was hardly the right setting for a Test match, but the crowd was remarkably well behaved. The only incidents were out in the middle on the mud track first used by Pakistan to make 246. They did well to reach that total, and it looked a winning score when we had replied with 139 for seven by the end of the second day, still 105 behind and with the unhealthy prospect of batting last on a crumbling wicket. Finger spinners Pervez, a left-armer, and off-spinner Saeed had brought about the collapse with only Graveney fighting them off in scoring 46.

Dolly was 16 not out at the close of play on that second day. Snow was his partner with myself and Cottam to come. Dolly's prospects of adding many more to his score were slim indeed that night, yet somehow he managed to add another 98 the next day to finish undefeated on 114 as well as finding time to encourage the rest of us to stay with him.

Snow lasted another 80 minutes while 40 were added for the eighth wicket. Snow scored nine. Then I managed to hold out for 70 minutes while 66 were added for the ninth wicket – only 22 of them to me. When I was out Dolly was still 20 short of his century but Cottam kept him partner while he reached three figures and steered us to a completely unexpected 28 run lead. The last three wickets had added 144 runs, just 35 of them contributed by Snow, Cottam and myself. In all Dolly batted 265 minutes for his 114 and gave just two difficult chances. A skilled craftsman at work in saving the match.

I find it difficult to decide whether this century was his finest for England, or the one on that rain-affected wicket at Christchurch in 1971. The wicket was going more in Christchurch, but this time Dolly had more reliable partners to come when he started his innings with us at 31 for three in reply to New Zealand's 65.

There was Hampshire who helped Dolly put on 64, and Illingworth was with him while 93 were added for the fifth wicket. In addition to his technique in combating a ball which turned and lifted spitefully every now and again, Dolly showed impeccable judgement in selecting which ball to hit. His century took him three and half hours, which is a respectable time these days on a good track.

Perhaps the most attacking innings I saw him play was the one against South Australia at Adelaide a couple of months before – again to save his side from certain defeat. That seemed the only possible outcome on the last day, with South Australia holding a 397 run advantage when we started our second innings. Getting the runs was out of the question, and survival the only hope when we lost our first seven wickets for 149. Dolly was 16 when Shuttleworth went to join him at that score. He was 64 when Shuttleworth was caught by Greg Chappell against the off-spin of Barry Richards, who was spending a season with South Australia and menacing us every time we came up against him. He scored 224 in one match and 146 in the next.

We were 220 for eight, still 177 behind, when I went out to join Dolly with ninety minutes left for play and only Willis to come. In those ninety minutes Dolly added 98 to finish on 162 not out, while I managed only 13 out of a partnership worth 116. In just under four hours he hit 22 fours without giving the slightest chance. Again he seldom allowed the South Australia bowlers to get a sight of me. One can only wonder what his record might have been if he had been able to play Test cricket before he reached his middle thirties.

I don't think there can be any greater tribute to a player than to say he has been desperately missed since his Test career ended against the Australians in 1972. The balance of the England attack has not really been right since then, and I know from talking with Illingworth that if the selectors had not been so determined to try and find a couple of younger players during 1973 against the New Zealanders, Illingworth would still have had Dolly in the side.

Earlier I wrote that if you break Dolly's ability down into sections he would not be top of the list as a batsman, bowler or fielder. Topping the list of the best batsmen I have bowled to must be Sobers, and I've already explained how he kept me waiting almost nine years for his wicket.

I have suffered in many Test matches against him when bowling for England, but it was in a championship match that he produced the most incredible innings I have seen. This was Sobers with a difference. A rare moment when he was motivated by anger.

The cause of his anger was the caution of Alan Dixon, skippering Kent that day, in setting Nottinghamshire a target. This was at Dover in 1968, Sobers' first season in championship cricket, and many other captains that summer found themselves in Alan's predicament. I could understand the problem. Just how did you allow for Sobers' brilliance when setting Nottinghamshire a run chase?

Not even Sobers was going to succeed in every innings. But if he came good, he could make the near impossible look easy. If he failed then the target would be well beyond the capabilities of the other Notts players. I'm sure that in the first couple of seasons the presence of Sobers proved to be an embarrassment on occasions rather than a help from Nottinghamshire's point of view. They must often have been asked to do the impossible just because Sobers was playing.

Alan Dixon, who was a good captain, tactically almost in the Yorkshire mould of not giving the opposition too much room unless he stood a chance of winning himself, decided that his way out on the last day of the championship match was to let the Kent second innings run its full course. We had scored 235 in our first innings, to which Nottinghamshire had replied with 228 for seven, and we made 178 the second time around before our innings closed.

Gary obviously felt we might have declared some twenty minutes or so earlier. By the time our innings ended Nottinghamshire were left with 135 minutes to score 186. Alan had one further reason for allowing the Kent second innings to go on longer than Sobers liked. John Dye had broken down the previous day and was unfit to bowl. But in view of the mood Sobers was in I doubt if even John Dye would have made any difference.

In the Nottinghamshire first innings Sobers had batted at number seven. This time he came in number three when Nottinghamshire were 38 for one, and from that moment the match was lost. With two sixes and 18 fours Sobers made 108 out of 148 in seventy-seven minutes, and Nottinghamshire cruised home by five wickets with twenty minutes to spare. This was the fastest century that summer, to round off a great match for him during which he also captured eleven wickets for the first time in his career.

He hit so powerfully through the line of the ball, off both front and back foot, that it was a treat to watch. But my greatest memory is of the number of times he swept against me and Alan, middling the ball every time. There was one incident in particular which stands out in my mind, when he stepped down the wicket against Alan and drove him with all his power.

The ball rocketed down the other end, sent one stump cartwheeling out of the ground to be expertly caught by umpire 'Lofty' Herman. From there the ball rebounded, still travelling at quite a pace, to the feet of Sobers who casually picked it up and tossed it back to Dixon standing at the end of his follow through.

I don't think I have ever seen such a look of astonishment as the one which flickered across Alan's face at that moment.

When Gary was on form I don't think there was any bowler who could hope to keep him quiet. He had every stroke and was equally strong off front and back foot. He seemed to pick up the line of the ball so early, and be in position to play his shot before anybody else. He swept as safely as is possible with that stroke and was tremendously strong through the off side. He timed his shots almost as well as Colin, but whereas Cowdrey, against the faster bowlers, stroked the ball to the boundary, Sobers still hit it with tremendous power. I don't recall the particular match but I do remember him hitting one straight back at me. My first reaction was to stick out my hand – but I quickly withdrew it in the nick of time. I hate to think of the damage the ball would have caused if I had left my hand there.

Not only have I the greatest admiration for Sobers as a player but I have the utmost respect for him as a person.

An illustration of Sobers the person occurred during the Edgbaston Test against the West Indies in 1973, one of the worst Tests for atmosphere and feeling in which I have played. Much of it was sparked off when the West Indies claimed a catch against Boycott and Kanhai showed his displeasure when umpire Arthur Fagg gave Boycott not out.

As a result of Kanhai's actions, Fagg refused to stand the next morning until he had received an apology. In the same match I thought Sobers got a nick against me and all the close in fielders went up immediately. Knotty swears to this day that Sobers touched it, but he was given not out.

That evening both teams attended an official function and Sobers deliberately looked for me. The incident obviously played on his mind for he said to me, 'I didn't hit the ball, I'm sure I didn't. If I thought I had done I'd have walked.' I admired him for that and I'm sure he would have done.

I saw that side of him again in the West Indies during the following winter after the running out of Kallicharran by Greig when the West Indies left-hander failed to ground his bat after I had bowled the final delivery of the day.

I am told that Sobers' first reaction was one of anger, yet he stayed at the ground for two hours after the close of play to escort Greig through the angry crowd to the car waiting to take him back to the hotel. At that stage the Trinidad crowd had still not been informed of the agreement to reverse the decision of umpire Douglas Sang Hue, and feelings were still running high. Whether Sobers had volunteered to act as Greig's escort or whether he had been asked to do so by the West Indies Board officials doesn't matter. The fact that he did so showed, in my opinion, the type of person he is.

I can well understand Sir Don Bradman going into raptures about Sobers after watching him score 254 in six hours for the Rest of the World against Australia in Melbourne. Sir Don said it was the best innings ever seen in Australia. I have never seen the new ball taken apart so savagely as Sobers did, with the help of Clive Lloyd, when playing for the Rest of the World against England at Edgbaston, in 1970.

There were just ninety minutes to go on the second day when Sobers came in to join Lloyd. The score was then 175 for four. By the close it was 296 for four with both batsmen in their sixties. In those ninety minutes they added 121 runs, 95 of them in the final hour, and the most outrageous spurt came when we took the new ball with half an hour to go. Time for just six overs of Snow and Brown, but they went for 47 runs, mostly off poor Brown. In his first over Brown was hit for a gigantic six over mid-on by Sobers. Lloyd was brilliant but he looked like a labourer in that last hour compared to the craftsman at the other end.

Lord's seemed to bring out the best in Sobers. Earlier in that summer he scored 183 for the Rest of the World against England, and in 1973 helped end Illingworth's reign as England captain when joining with Bernard Julien in putting on 155 in two hours in the final Test.

After 157 from Kanhai the West Indies were already well placed when Sobers started on his 150 not out to boost the West Indies to 652 for eight, their highest total in England. Not only was Sobers murderous with the bat, he was a tremendous help to Julien that afternoon. Julien is a truly gifted player who, when he has learned to put all his strokes together, will be a world class player, and we are extremely fortunate to have him at Kent.

He has not really learned to play an innings yet, possibly due to lack of opportunity with Kent, but when he joined Sobers at the wicket, Sobers steered him through the afternoon to make sure Julien reached three figures, his first century in first class cricket. Whenever Julien showed any signs of losing his concentration, Sobers had a quiet word with him and steered him through.

Rohan Kanhai produced an innings against me which compares favourably with that d'Oliveira century on the wet wicket at Christchurch. This time the setting was Gravesend in 1970, on a wicket offering erratic and considerable turn from the first morning. A wicket on which I am expected to bowl Kent to victory without too much trouble. In fact I took 14 wickets in the game – seven in each Warwickshire innings – but finished on the losing side. Kanhai was responsible, with the support of Amiss.

His innings on that first day was an education, his judgement flawless in scoring 107 in just over three hours. He came in after I had had Jameson caught for four, and sent my first ball hurtling over long-on for six. It was the first of three he hit off me.

Throughout those three hours he played on a line with his stumps. In other words, when the ball was going to miss the stumps he didn't follow it, as most batsmen would instinctively have done. He played each ball as if it were straight, so that when it turned it beat the edge of the bat. And when the ball took off, he just gently dropped his wrists to allow it to go over his bat. But whenever I dropped one fractionally short or overpitched, he was on it like a flash. Whether I dropped that first ball a little short, and so gave him room to take a step down the wicket, or whether he made up his mind to strike a psychological blow by belting it straightaway, I just don't know. But whatever the reason it gave him great confidence.

One batsman who watched and learned from Kanhai's innings that day was Amiss, then batting in the middle order. He partnered Kanhai for a while in the first innings and then reproduced the Kanhai bad wicket technique in making 91 in the second before driving a return catch to me. The wicket had eased by then but was still awkward. Like Kanhai, Amiss, after a nervous start, played very straight. Stuart Leary, with his unorthodox style and keen eye, was the only Kent batsman to offer resistance against Warwickshire in our defeat.

It was against Warwickshire on another dodgy wicket that I saw one of the finest innings played by a Kent batsman during my early years in county cricket. It was in my first season, in fact, when we played at Nuneaton in conditions where the ball was seaming alarmingly as well as lifting sharply. The odds looked heavily stacked against us when Alan Brown bowled Warwickshire out for 104 in their second innings, taking eight for 47. He was virtually unplayable, the majority of the runs he conceded coming from edges and nicks, with the Warwickshire batsmen having little idea where the ball was going.

We were left to score 189 in four hours fifty minutes. So time was not important. Anyway, we doubted whether we would last a couple of hours. As far as Warwickshire were concerned it was simply a question of how many runs they would win by, especially as they had Tom Cartwright in their side, and the conditions were ideal for him to exploit as only he can.

Not only did we last two hours, but that was all the time we needed to win by ten wickets, with Peter Richardson playing a blinding innings of 139. He needed a little luck at the start, when he offered a couple of hard chances before he had reached double figures. But from then on he was in charge while Luckhurst gave him support in scoring 46. Richardson was at his most audacious against the leg spin of Barber, sweeping him continually round the corner. In the end Barber had two men back on the boundary for the sweep, but still Richardson was bisecting them. He demonstrated his complete mastery of the conditions in one over against Cartwright when he struck him for five successive boundaries. This probably made Barber feel a little better for he was taken off after his nine overs had cost 49 runs.

I have already mentioned that Suttle always made runs against us when we played Sussex, even the odd double century. Another was Dexter. The first time I played against him was at Hastings in 1963, and he scored a century overflowing with superb drives. He and Jim Parks, another century maker during their first innings 338 for six, took us apart on a well-grassed wicket, but Dexter was so elegant and brilliant in the execution of his strokes that he took the eye even when Parks outscored him for a while.

The following summer Dexter scored another century for Sussex against us, and almost made it a hat-trick in 1966. That was an embarrassing match for me. He had started his innings that day just before the close of play and I missed an easy catch against him off Dixon before he had made double figures. Dixon pulled my leg in the dressing-room afterwards and said, 'Now you can bowl at the b—— when he's got 50.' I did too, and also when he was approaching his century. Dexter was only three or four runs short when he was caught.

The innings I recall best, however, was in 1968 when he took one look at the England batting against Australia in that summer and suddenly decided to make a come-back. He announced he would be available for England if they wanted him, but obviously the selectors had to be convinced he had lost none of his golden touch. It was Kent's misfortune that Sussex's next match happened to be against us at Hastings.

There is normally a fairly healthy crowd at Hastings for these battles, but even more had been attracted by Dexter's first championship appearance since he had announced his retirement from full time cricket two years previously. They came to see him bat and were not disappointed when Mike Griffith, leading Sussex for the first time, won the toss. The spectators did not have to wait long either. The wicket was damp and Sussex lost three for 17. Within half an hour of the start Dexter was walking in to bat. And there he stayed. The way he got out was by having a slog at 6.25, thinking the close was 6.30. Nobody had told him play was going on to seven, or else he would surely have stayed on and made his highest score in first class cricket.

As it was he finished only two short of his career best of 205 for England against Pakistan in Karachi. The way he played he might easily have been back on that dead Karachi wicket again instead of a damp Hastings track offering us some help. In those five and half hours at the crease he scored 203 runs, hit three sixes and 23 fours. He was 180 when the clock showed 6.20 and decided to slog to reach his double hundred before what he thought was the close. In the next over against Dixon he hit him for six, four, six, four and three and was still attempting to hit out when driving a catch to Dixon in the next over off me. That was enough for the selectors. They named him the next day to return for England.

Thanks to the wonderful standard of Kent fielding, particularly in recent years, and the number of safe hands we have had close to the wicket, there have not been many batsmen able to really take the Kent bowling apart. Centuries, yes, but few really explosive innings. There are always a few batsmen who seem to do well against us, like John Edrich, but he has had to work for his runs.

I've been very fortunate to have played for a side whose ability in the field has been so high. Colin Cowdrey at slip for instance, Alan Dixon in the covers, Mike Denness, Asif and Alan Ealham anywhere. Stuart Leary was a fine close-to-the-wicket catcher, Luckhurst has been one of the most outstanding backward short legs I have seen, and Bob Woolmer does a good job for us at short square today.

We are better today than we were ten years ago, but we were still pretty useful then. Not that Graeme Pollock gave us much chance to shine in 1965 except in the art of retrieving the ball from the boundary. His innings that day for South Africa against Kent at Canterbury was another of the classics I recall with great clarity.

He scored 203 not out in 240 minutes, his second century taking just an hour. He enjoyed century partnerships with first Ali Bacher and then Colin Bland, offering only one clearcut chance which Cowdrey, of all people, put down in the slips when 76. That apart, Graeme was superb in the classic, orthodox style, a model for any schoolboy in the way he stood up and hit the ball straight, obtaining many of his runs in the arc between mid-off and mid-on. In all he scored 142 runs from boundary strokes.

At the time the South Africans were feeling very pleased with themselves having defeated England 1–0 in the three match series, the victory achieved at Trent Bridge when Pollock made a century in two hours. It was a great pity we had to wait until the 1970 Rest of the World series before we were able to see Pollock in action again in a first class contest. That Canterbury match contains other memories for me. I had a 'king pair', the second time being the third victim in a hat-trick.

The centuries by the Chappell brothers at the Oval in 1972 were a marvellous performance, Ian being the more rugged type of player, Greg more the artist. There is quite a contrast in styles when they bat and they each have their own individual weaknesses. Ian is a little suspect against pace bowling and attempts to bluster his way through it when he first comes in. He is a far from safe hooker despite his claims that he has now solved the problem. If I were a fast bowler I would always fancy myself against him early in his innings.

As a spinner I find him quite difficult to bowl to because he uses his feet so well, and is a tremendously strong cutter of the ball – like many overseas players – when given the chance. When I drop one a little short against him it usually goes for four. Greg is the opposite. I don't think he fancies spin bowling when he first comes in and would much rather find his feet against the faster bowlers. Like Graeme Pollock, he plays it straight and must now be numbered among the top half dozen middle order batsmen in the world.

On a par with that great century at the Oval was his first innings in Test cricket against us at Perth in the second Test of the 1970–71 tour. He scored a hundred on that occasion, too. It was an innings of character for he was given a hard time when he first came in, and after forty minutes had been restricted to a single. Australia were also struggling at the time on 107 for five in answer to our 397 – a total which owes a lot to a century from Luckhurst.

The taking of the second new ball gave Greg Chappell the chance to show his stroke-making quality even though Snow was pretty lethal at the time. Once he started scoring he just went faster and faster, and in the first hour after tea that day raced from 48 to three figures. I rated that performance highly, probably because I did not suffer. I had been dropped for that Test.

Watching Test matches has made me appreciate the qualities of Geoff Boycott and the tremendous burden he has had to bear over the last ten years as England's opening batsman. He has been the one constant factor – at least up until the last couple of seasons – while selectors have turned from one partner to another through Bob Barber, Colin Milburn, Eric Russell, John Edrich, Brian Luckhurst, Dennis Amiss and others who have made the odd Test appearances from time to time.

A Boycott century lacks the appeal of one by Pollock, Sobers, Richards, Kanhai, Greg Chappell and others as far as spectators are concerned, but watching him at work is a fascinating experience and makes one appreciate the sheer technical brilliance of his performances. Like a great actor playing his favourite part, in each of his innings Geoff seems to follow the same pattern, reducing risks to a minimum until he is ready to deliver his pay-off line – his century – revealed predictably like the culprit on the last page of an Agatha Christie thriller.

He has got everything so worked out that I have found him

relatively easy to bowl to and keep in check. He is waiting for me to make a mistake, while I try to lure him into a false stroke. Mind you, he always complains that he usually meets me on a wicket helping the bowler and I must confess he is right. 'Wait till I get you on a good 'un,' he says to me quite frequently.

Ken Barrington was another of a similar type. Seldom devastating at the crease but utterly dependable, he saved England time and again. He, too, carried a tremendous burden as the anchor man at a time when England's middle order batting was suspect in the 1960s. I have already spoken of Tom Graveney's brilliant return to the England side in 1966, when he scored a century in my first Test match, and I can remember him coming out on top in another sound display which has no place in the record books.

It took place in the nets at Dacca, East Pakistan, on the 1968–69 tour. He was vice-captain of that party under Colin, and annoyed John Snow just before the first of the three Test series in Lahore. In the final net session John had been relaxing, bowling gentle left arm deliveries when Tom and Colin asked him to bowl a few deliveries flat out to convince them of his fitness after we had been confined to our hotel for three days because of rioting in the town centre.

Both Colin and Tom asked John to bowl properly but he still persisted in taking things easy. He felt he was fit enough, didn't want to exhaust himself in the dry heat, and must have felt sure of his Test place. Not having seen him bowl for about a week the selectors decided to leave him out of the first Test side and John was obviously annoyed when he was told. He blamed Tom for their decision. . . .

The next time John got a ball in his hand was at the net sessions immediately before the second Test of the series in Dacca. The nets had been watered that morning, and although the sun came out strongly to dry them they were unfit when Tom went into bat. John decided to prove to Tom that he was fit to play. He sent down some real screamers which bounced and lifted, but Tom played them all as if he were on a good, hard wicket, thanked John for his bowling and walked out of the net completely unruffled. It was a marvellous exhibition of how to handle fast bowling. Tom knew exactly what John was trying to do but he played it well and never flinched.

That tour saw the last Test innings of Colin Milburn, who was flown over from Perth where he had been playing for Western Australia to join an MCC party hard hit by injuries. Besides being the last Test innings by Milburn, it was also one of his most impressive. He was to lose the sight of his left eye in a road accident soon after he returned to England.

I have a great affection for Colin. He was making his mark with Northants about the same time I was starting with Kent, and we were often bracketed together by the cricket writers as two of England's hopes for the future. We roomed together when I made my Test debut at Trent Bridge, and I saw another side of Milburn on the eve of the Test.

Until then I had known him as a happy-go-lucky character always ready for a laugh and a joke, a love of life which shone through in his cricket. That night he was as nervous as I was. In the second innings of the second Test at Lord's he had smashed the West Indies bowling, including Hall and Griffith, all around the ground when making a quickfire 126 not out. Now he was worried about what Hall and Griffith were going to do to him at Trent Bridge.

'They're bound to be after me after that lot at Lord's. They'll be out to get me this time,' he said time and again that evening.

Milburn had been through another good season with Western Australia when he arrived to join us in riot-torn Pakistan, instead of spending three weeks at sea with Graham McKenzie sailing home to England. He arrived too late to play in the second Test at Dacca but went into the side for the third and final match at Karachi. It was quite a transformation for him. One week he was playing on the fast wickets of Perth with their high degree of bounce, and the next he was going out on the slow, sluggish wicket of Karachi, with hardly any bounce at all.

This is why I say his innings of 139, interrupted at various stages by demonstrations – some political, others calling for Hanif to be reinstated as Pakistan captain in place of Saeed Ahmed – was one of his finest. There were no Milburn fireworks, no indiscriminate hitting which had labelled him a risky player whenever he had appeared for England before. Instead he waited for the right ball to hit – usually the short one which he smashed square on the off or pulled over mid-wicket – while being content to score his ones and twos in between.

It was a performance which indicated he had learned to build an innings and to bat with discretion – the two qualities he needed to go with his stroke-making ability to become a regular Test opener for England.

What a great tragedy he never had the chance to hold down that place.

7. THE ART OF CAPTAINCY

Illingworth, the best of them all? . . . Regaining the Ashes after thirty years . . . A captain's problems, on and off the field . . . My experience of England captains . . . And some from abroad.

During the last three summers that Ray Illingworth led the England side many people asked me what was wrong between us. The answer is straightforward and simple – nothing.

The question was posed because during that period I was left out of the England side more times than I was selected. Of the seventeen Test matches played at home in that period I played in eight and Norman Gifford was preferred as the left-arm spinner in the other nine. And I played in one of those only because Gifford was injured.

Some cricket writers even suggested that Ray and I were not on the same wavelength because he was not selecting me – the same cricket writers who were being critical of my failure to get among the wickets on good pitches. If I failed to strike they were saying I was ineffective and yet, when I was left out of the Test side, they wrote that they were surprised the selectors had dropped me.

The question became so persistent that in the end I began to think there was something behind it. At the next opportunity I tackled Ray and asked him exactly where I stood as far as Test cricket was concerned and how he felt about my bowling.

He told me: 'On good wickets I don't think there is anything to choose between you and Gifford. On a wicket doing something I would rather have you in my side.' That, as far as I was concerned, was fair enough. One of the qualities I admired about Illingworth. He was always honest and straightforward with his team and you knew exactly where you stood with him.

That brief conversation told me all I wanted to know. Ray had nothing against me and I certainly had nothing against him. In fact I rate him as probably the best captain I have served under.

Illingworth's success in regaining the Ashes in Australia on the 1970–71 tour is one important reason why I place him ahead of the others. When a captain has led his side into achieving something which had not been done for almost thirty years, his players must think he has something extra about him.

One quality I liked about Illingworth was the same I found in Basil d'Oliveira's batting. Illingworth always appeared to be in control whatever the situation. It was a most comforting thought. He gave us all tremendous confidence, especially in the final Test at Sydney.

After the first day it seemed obvious that the match was going to produce an outright result. To regain the Ashes, after taking a 1–0 lead in the series on our first visit to Sydney, meant we had to win the final Test as well. Even when the situation may have appeared a little grim to outsiders, we all felt that Ray was going to lead us home. He did not let us down.

Illingworth has gained a reputation for being one of the shrewdest judges in the game, with a flair for picking the right answer to see us through any crisis. But playing under Colin Cowdrey for Kent and England, I can say that Colin was just as shrewd. He missed very little.

Illingworth never gave the impression of being at all indecisive. He seemed to know exactly where he was going with every step he took, every decision he made.

He was marvellous in building up the pressure and tension on the opposing batsmen, and getting them to crack under the strain even when their victory target seemed just around the corner. That suits me, of course, for this is exactly the procedure I adopt when bowling on a good wicket. I could understand exactly what Illingworth was doing.

Most of the time he was forced to operate that way because he seldom had runs to play with when he was England's captain. The batting may not have been as strong as many captains would have liked, but Illingworth preferred to have the extra bowler to call upon, the greater the variety the better. He felt that bowlers, not batsmen, won matches.

The situation was very tight against the West Indies at Headingley in 1969 in the third Test when they started their second innings needing 303 to win to level the series, and appeared to be three quarters of the way there at 219 for four. Ray never panicked. He changed his attack around until he found the right combination and squeezed out a victory.

Another one which seemed lost on the final day was against Pakistan on the same ground in 1971, but again Ray produced a 25 run victory when Pakistan, on 160 for five, appeared to be heading for their victory, needing 231 to win on an easy wicket. I wasn't playing in that match but the boys who were never thought England would lose.

But Sydney and the final Test of the Australian tour was Ray's greatest day, considering that we had gone into the match without Boycott and then lost Snow. Boycott had broken an arm a few days before when batting against Graham McKenzie, and John Snow ran into a boundary fence, making a mess of his right hand, just after the Australian second innings had started. He had bowled only two overs before Illingworth was robbed of the bowler who had caused the Australian batsmen to jerk around like uncontrollable puppets.

It was a dicey situation. Batting first, we had made only 184 and the Australians had taken an 80 run first innings lead. With Luckhurst and Edrich both scoring half centuries in a 94 run opening partnership, we batted much better in our second innings and ended up by setting the Australians the score of 223 to win. This was less than Ray wanted. He would have preferred something more like 300 to feel safe. But he took it all in his stride when Snow's injury threatened to destroy us at the last moment.

When the final day started the Australians were still in with a good chance, needing exactly 100 to draw the series. They had five wickets left, including those of Greg Chappell, who emerged as their major batsman on the tour, and the belligerent Rodney Marsh. They were the two not out batsmen which still left them with O'Keeffe and Jenner, no novices with the bat.

Ray handled everything so well on that last morning that there was never any danger of us losing. In 95 minutes it was all over, the last five wickets having gone down for the addition of 37 runs that day, leaving us winners by 62 runs. Illingworth didn't miss

Caught Underwood (D), bowled Underwood (K). I take a catch at short leg off the bowling of my elder brother Keith, playing for local club side Beckenham.

The season is over and I get a chance to relax with my wife Dawn.

With my mother and father who have given me so much help and encouragement throughout my career.

Not the classic way to play the bouncer perhaps but the most effective method I can manage. At least it worked on this occasion.

How the left-handed batsman usually sees me as I come up to bowl over the wicket. Normally I bowl round the wicket to right-handers.

Up past umpire David Constant, a former Kent colleague, showing a sideways view of my action.

Colin Cowdrey awarding me my county cap during Kent's match against the Australians at Canterbury in 1964.

Dennis Amiss in action against Pakistan in 1974 showing the power which took him to a double century against the West Indies in Jamaica in his match-saving epic earlier in the year. I partnered him for almost two hours.

Basil d'Oliveira strikes again and there is no catching this ball. Basil was my partner in my first Test innings at Trent Bridge and became my 'Mr Cricket'.

Bishen Bedi, the India and Northamptonshire left-arm spinner whose style I've been encouraged to follow.

Brian Close's appointment as England captain in 1966 resulted in me losing my Test place but I still rate him as one of the finest leaders I have known.

Ray Illingworth was my first victim in first-class cricket. Test spinning partner and England captain—the best I served under.

My Kent captain Mike Denness who faced a tough challenge as England captain against the West Indies in 1974, but we squared the series.

Colin Cowdrey, captain of Kent when I joined the county and one of the most influential figures on my career. I shall always be grateful.

Wicketkeeper Jackie Hendriks can't bear to look, but other West Indies players rush to my aid after being felled by a bouncer from Charlie Griffith on my Test debut at Nottingham in 1966.

Leaving the field at Headingley in 1968 after making 45 against the Australians in the Fourth Test, my highest Test score to the end of the 1974 season. David Brown and I added 61 for the last wicket.

With only six minutes to go John Inverarity makes a mistake, the match is over, Australia beaten and the series squared at the Oval in 1968 in the most sensational Test finish of my career.

a trick as captain, and bowled magnificently in taking three for 39 in twenty controlled overs of off-spin. I managed two wickets on that last morning and d'Oliveira came on, just when O'Keeffe was threatening to hit out, to ease out the tail with two wickets in five overs. I got the final wicket when Jenner presented a catch to Fletcher at short leg, and the Ashes had been regained. A wicket and a moment I shall never forget.

The timing of Illingworth's bowling changes was immaculate and so was his choice of bowler to suit the batsman. He was very good for me, kidding the Australians that I was turning the ball dangerously by giving me two close catchers, even when I was struggling to move the ball off the straight.

In the previous Test at Sydney Illingworth pulled off a master stroke to help England to victory. It happened right at the start of the third day, when Australia were 189 for four in their first innings in reply to our 332. The previous night Ian Redpath (64) and Doug Walters (55) had been going well. They were Australia's main hopes when play resumed on that third morning. The new ball was not far away, which prevented Ray from opening up with a burst from Snow, Willis or Lever, and at the same time gave the batsmen a chance to settle in.

Everybody expected Illingworth to open up himself, with me as his partner. Instead he threw the ball to d'Oliveira, who had Redpath caught in the slips playing inside his first ball of the day. I am sure that Redpath was as surprised as everybody to find d'Oliveira bowling to him when he must have tuned himself mentally to facing Illingworth.

That innings was my most successful of the series in terms of figures, and I finished with four for 66. I'd taken a return catch to dismiss Greg Chappell the previous day, and followed up by claiming the wickets of Stackpole – batting in the middle order – Marsh and Mallett as Australia were put out for 236.

An undefeated 142 by Boycott in our second innings enabled Ray to declare on 319 for five, and Australia were shot out for 116 in their second innings by some inspired bowling by Snow, who took seven for 40.

Illingworth looked after his players' interests. He was always willing to tackle the authorities on their behalf if any of them had any grouse, and insisted on the best for his team when some of the rules laid down made things difficult. He saw to it that many of the minor irritations were removed. But he was not the ideal choice as captain in the eyes of many people, particularly when it came to handling the social duties which captains are expected to carry out on tours. These functions were not Illingworth's scene, and I sympathize with his attitude to a certain extent. He was in Australia to play cricket. His mission was to beat the Australians and not perform as an after-dinner speaker.

If Illingworth had a fault it was in being too honest and approachable, particularly with the press. When they asked a leading question he gave an honest answer instead of ducking the issue with a more diplomatic reply. He might have been a little more selective in his choice of words, but that is his way.

However, I can understand why Ray took us off the field in that final Test match when beer cans and bottles were tossed on the field, even if the manner of Ray's leaving upset some people. You can't play cricket in that atmosphere. I don't agree with those who criticized Ray when he sent Snow to field on the boundary where he was a target for a few noisy spectators. These had been upset when Jenner had ducked into a delivery from Snow just short of a length.

Illingworth had every right to place his fielders where he wanted them and I don't think he was guilty of acting without thought when he allowed Snow to take up his usual position at the end of the over. He showed every consideration to me once when the spectators were having a go after I'd dropped an easy chance off Walters. I was fielding on the boundary just in front of the famous Sydney Hill when I was slow in getting into position to take the catch at third man.

For a few minutes the Hill crowd gave me a hard time, and Illingworth immediately put me in another position away from that boundary area. He did not want my confidence affected in any way. I'm sure he would not have sent Snow to the boundary if he had expected any trouble.

Illingworth's clashes with umpire Lou Rowan, the senior Australian umpire, also caused a great deal of controversy during the tour. Ray possibly over-reacted at times, but he had cause, considering some of the decisions which went against us. Rowan, in my opinion, found the pressure too much for him in the end and cracked under the strain. Pressure was telling on us all when the schedule was rearranged to produce twenty days' tense Test cricket out of thirty-nine.

Rowan was given a rough time by the Australian cricket writers in particular. It all started in the first Test at Brisbane when he gave Keith Stackpole not out after Boycott had hit the stumps with a direct throw as the batsmen went for a quick single. Stackpole was then 18 and went on to make 175. A cameraman had snapped the incident and the picture clearly showed Stackpole's bat short of the crease at the moment a bail was sent flying.

The picture was widely used throughout Australia, and from that moment every incident and not out verdict given by Rowan was played up. I suffered on more than one occasion, after appeals for catches were turned down when I was convinced the batsman had hit the ball. In some cases there was no other way to explain the amount of deviation. I am not calling into question Rowan's honesty. The Stackpole run out in the first Test was a desperately close thing, and I am sure Rowan gave an honest answer in his own mind – and continued to do so throughout the tour. Personally I found him an extremely charming man, but it would have been a miracle if any umpire could have stood the pressure he was under during the series. It could not have been pleasant for him to see the headline in a newspaper, 'Rowan blunders again', as he must have done on more than one occasion.

Neither would I like the problems of a manager. It is a thankless task and it must be difficult for the Test and County Cricket Board to find a captain and manager who are compatible.

My view is that a tour overseas must be a captain's show. He is the guiding light, closely followed by the manager, whose duties, in my opinion, should be restricted to the handling of travel, hotel and all financial aspects. These two should be operating very much together, and the manager should not overstep his line of responsibility and enter into the playing side. I'm not 100 per cent in favour of the tour manager being in on Test selection meetings either.

The best combination I have come across was on the 1972–73 tour of India and Pakistan when Donald Carr, now secretary of the Test and County Cricket Board, was manager, while Tony Lewis was given the opportunity to become the regular England captain. They got on well together, both had the complete support of the players, and it became the happiest MCC party with which I have travelled. There was only one thing lacking in the end: we did not win either series.

Tony was a charmer. Lively, full of fun, marvellous off the field and determined on it. He had not got quite the tactical appreciation of the other England captains with whom I have served, but was most approachable in every way.

I had a very nice letter from him when the tour party was selected, saying how much he was looking forward to working with me, and he wrote another letter when we arrived home thanking me for my efforts. Typical of what I had been accustomed to under Colin Cowdrey, and it was much appreciated by the players.

Tony tried very hard on that tour, although I think he was having fitness problems with his knee. This might have been the reason why he did not score as many runs as the selectors were hoping for in their need to find somebody to replace Illingworth, even though he produced a couple of very good innings in the Tests. As I wrote earlier, he lacked Illingworth's tactical experience which was a serious handicap against India on a wicket taking spin. But it was a pleasure to play for him all the same.

He was always very easy to approach with suggestions, and he was as honest with his players as Illingworth. There was no beating about the bush, no offering of lame excuses when someone was left out of the side, as I have known with some captains. When I was dropped for the last Test of the tour against Pakistan in Karachi Tony came to see me in my hotel room and said: 'Hard luck, Deadly. It was a very close thing but we've decided to give Jack Birkenshaw a go this time, and Norman Gifford stays in as well. We think that Birkenshaw's style will be better suited to this wicket.'

That was fair enough. Gifford had been bowling well and nobody could argue with the reasoning put forward for including Birkenshaw. Tony didn't try to offer any excuses. He just summed up the situation and was completely honest. That's all I ask from a captain. I think a player should always be told by the captain himself whether he has been dropped or selected rather than learn it from an outside source, as has happened on tour. I'd much prefer that at the end of a selection meeting all the players were summoned and told then and there before the press were informed.

Colin, of course, was very easy to approach and always ready to listen. Not only did he listen but he gave you your head. Many people have described him as a defensive captain, but I always felt with Colin that I knew exactly what he was doing. There was never an in-between situation. I knew when he was attacking and when he was defending.

When he was attacking, particularly against a new batsman, I thought Colin's field placings were masterly, better than those set by Illingworth. He had everything just right so that, as long as the bowler kept his line and length, he could pin a new batsman down and really make him struggle to get off the mark.

He always had the right mixture of close-in fielders, as well as the others further back to save the runs. When Illingworth attacked I sometimes felt he put too many around the bat, allowing the batsman the chance of getting off the mark with one off the edge. Nothing is more upsetting for a bowler.

Colin was absolutely brilliant at dangling the carrot so that the other side became interested in a run chase. Sometimes he struggled within himself before making up his mind he could win a match. But once he reached that decision he wasn't often thwarted. In setting the opposition a run target, he made sure they were duty-bound to go for the runs the whole time.

He used the brake and then the accelerator in the most subtle way, like a Grand Prix racing driver nursing his car around a twisting circuit in wet weather. If the opposition made a bad start, he would give them runs without them really noticing it, so that the target was always tempting. If they got too far advanced he could put on the brake. When there was a danger of the opposition calling off the run chase because they had lost too many wickets, he would put them back in the picture. He won many, many games for Kent that way.

Obviously it was a great blow to him when he failed to get the captaincy for the 1970–71 tour of Australia, for what would be his last MCC tour there. It was most unfortunate that he snapped that Achilles tendon when he did, early in 1969, thus ruling himself out of cricket for the rest of that season. It was Illingworth's good fortune, however, that he was given the England captaincy and made a good job of it that summer. Colin did go as Ray's vice-captain and little did we realise that Colin would in fact go to Australia yet again on the 1974–75 tour.

In 1968 Colin tried to set a new trend for the first Test at Old Trafford against Australia, following his successful tour of the West Indies when he had won the series the previous winter. I missed that trip, but I gather the team spirit was marvellous and Colin was trying to keep it bubbling at home. It resulted in no less than fourteen players being named for that first Test.

Unfortunately, all this succeeded in doing was to give the selectors too many alternatives when it came to making up their minds on the final morning of the match. The trouble arose when Barrington pulled out through injury. This worried Colin. He wanted to play safe at that stage of the series and strengthen the batting as much as possible. He got his way, but I think we fielded an unbalanced team and lost the match.

David Brown, Tom Cartwright and myself were left out while Bob Barber, who had been out of Test cricket for some time and was not even playing regularly for Warwickshire, was selected for his leg-spinners and to bat number five. The fast bowlers were Snow and Higgs, supported by d'Oliveira, who never pretended to be a first change bowler. Pat Pocock was given the off-spinning role. The bowling just wasn't strong enough and we lost by 159 runs. Higgs, Barber, d'Oliveira and Pocock were all left out of the next match.

My experience of Close as England captain was limited to two Test matches in 1967 against Pakistan, but from that brief encounter I can understand why so many cricketers rate him highly. He had taken over from Colin for the last Test against the West Indies in 1966, and one of his first tasks was to drop me. I missed the three match series against India at the start of 1967 and the first against Pakistan before I was recalled.

People admire Close, not so much because of his considerable tactical ability, but the sheer personality of the man himself, his complete belief in England and English cricketers as the best in the world. Like Illingworth, he filled me with confidence, although for a different reason. To see him crouching at silly point, right in the firing line and never flinching, made you play for him.

The second occasion I was with him was the final Test of that 1967 summer. We had all reported for nets on the day Close was hauled before the MCC to be disciplined for alleged time-wasting in the Warwickshire–Yorkshire championship match at Edgbaston a few weeks earlier. He was found guilty and censured.

We had almost finished our net practice when Close was able to get away from Lord's and join us at the Oval. I shall never forget him coming up to us, one by one, to tell us of the verdict and then ask: 'Have you any objections playing under me in this match?' If one player had hesitated giving his answer then I am sure Close would have handed over the captaincy then and there. Nobody had the slightest objection and he had our complete backing for the match.

But the situation must have been difficult for him on the morning of the match, with the front and back pages of the newspapers detailing the findings of his 'court' case. The timing of that disciplinary meeting at Lord's could not have been worse. Entering a Test match provides enough tension on its own, without additional pressures being heaped on players, especially the captain.

As if that was not enough, he encountered another problem that morning when Boycott pulled out of the match with a throat infection, leaving England without an opener to partner Cowdrey at number two. When the time came for England to bat Close decided to take on the job himself rather than ask any other batsman to play out of order. I took my hat off to him that day as I watched him going out to bat. There, I thought to myself, goes a man.

My own county captain, Mike Denness, is the other leader under whom I have served for England, and even after the 1974–75 tour to Australia and New Zealand it is still difficult to judge him by Test standards. He had a tough baptism in the West Indies on the 1973–74 tour, but that was hardly a fair tour on which to pass judgement. It was a difficult assignment, taking over from the popular Illingworth when he had not even been a regular member of the Test side.

I'm sure he would be the first to admit that he found it hard going at first, especially after losing the first Test when unfair criticism was levelled against him. The following home series against India didn't require any outstanding leadership qualities, but those who played under him in the Caribbean and also served under him against Pakistan during the second half of the summer must have noticed a difference. Everybody should learn from experience, and Mike certainly learned. He had another difficulty at the start, to prove to everybody that he could hold a place as a batsman. And this he did against India.

Where I felt he was at a slight disadvantage at the start was in his lack of knowledge of how a bowler feels and thinks. Illingworth, Close and, to a certain extent, Cowdrey had this knowledge because of their bowling experience. Although Cowdrey did not bowl often he had done so as a youngster and turned his arm over in his early days of county cricket. Mike had no such background, but by the end of 1974 he was making up for it by consulting his bowlers regularly.

Mike's appointment as Kent captain has affected me in one way. I don't bowl as many overs now as I did under Cowdrey. Under Colin I would often be the first change bowler, and when I turned up to face a day in the field I knew I was going to bowl twenty or thirty overs. Nowadays we have a surplus of seam bowlers in the Kent side, and Mike is forced to try them before turning to me.

Of the Test captains I've played against I always had a high regard for the way Sobers handled his side. He always played the game in an attacking manner, which meant the crowd would enjoy the cricket too. But this did not always make him the most professional of captains. I think that this began to show in some of the West Indies results, when their high class side of the early and middle sixties began to break up towards the end of the decade.

Before then he could afford to give away a certain amount of runs and keep the game loose, safe in the knowledge that he had the batsmen capable of scoring more runs than the opposition nine times out of ten. If his batsmen couldn't do it for him there was always Sobers himself to turn the match. He often did.

When he lost Hunte, Butcher, Nurse and one or two others he did not have this batting. And when Hall and Griffith went at the same time, he did not possess the experienced bowlers to keep the opposition in check. Nottinghamshire might have also gained a few more victories over the years Sobers was in charge if he had been more professional in his captaincy. But then again he didn't play his cricket that way. That's why he was good for the game.

Bill Lawry is another charmer off the field, a very funny man with a good sense of humour, all of which he seemed to leave behind once he stepped over the boundary line and walked to the middle. He captained the side very much as he batted, solidly and defensively, and caused controversy everywhere he went by his 'non-walking' approach. I can see a great deal of commonsense in his argument that he would be given out from time to time when he wasn't out, so he might as well leave everything to the umpires and benefit from some not out decisions even when he knew he had nicked the ball. There is a lot to be said for adopting that practice, but surely it must also mean that the batsman has to accept the umpire's decision with good grace all the time. This Lawry failed to do at times.

He always amused me by his habit of taking off his batting gloves and leaving them out in the middle to dry whenever the players came off the field for lunch or tea breaks. It was as if he were reminding the crowd that although he wasn't out in the middle in person, he was still there in spirit.

As a leader Ian Chappell was a big improvement when he took over for the final Test of the 1970–71 series. He showed he was prepared to try the unexpected and be far more adventurous than Lawry in his use of the spinners. That wizard of spin, Johnny Gleeson, who used the unorthodox method of flicking the ball off his middle finger to impart the turn, would undoubtedly have been more successful if he had not played so many Tests under Lawry. The tall Victorian used Gleeson as a defensive bowler with defensive fields when his type cried out for an attacking policy. Few people could read Gleeson properly, certainly not on our tour. Boycott managed to work him out and so did d'Oliveira towards the end. Others adopted various methods to combat him, but all would have been in more serious trouble if Lawry had used Gleeson to attack us with fielders in close catching positions.

Despite the fact that Chappell was the more adventurous, and we had to win that final Test to take the Ashes, we were all relieved that Lawry was no longer our opponent. We would not have enjoyed facing him when Australia were starting their second innings wanting only 232 to win.

Ajit Wadekhar proved a very good leader when India beat England here in 1971, a sound man who gave his side inspiration when he was at the crease. He was still impressive when we visited India in 1972, but he failed over here in 1974. He wasn't in good form with the bat, and I don't think he was really given a chance, being sent here without an opening attack or any seam bowlers.

I thought Rohan Kanhai did a very good job in the West Indies on our tour and in England the previous summer, especially in the way he handled his bowlers. He was alive to everything in the field. But he was criticized in the West Indies for failing to bowl England out for a second time in Jamaica, where Amiss made that match-saving double century, and in Barbados where Fletcher scored a century on the last day. However, I thought the wickets were more at fault than Kanhai. In each match they just got better and better, slower and slower.

Intikhab, too, has looked a lively and aggressive captain in leading Pakistan to this country on two occasions.

What makes a good captain? It isn't really difficult. Strip away all the ballyhoo, the experience, the expertise, the shrewdness and everything else, and it all boils down to one simple fact. A winning captain is a good captain. And that largely depends on the ability of the players he has with him, the wicket conditions he finds himself playing on and a great deal of luck.

All winning captains are good captains – until they lose.

8. ON TOUR—AND ON SHOW

Passed over for the West Indies tour, 1967–68 . . . Round Africa and the East with Mickey Stewart . . . Cricketers, or Ambassadors? . . . The pleasures and pains of going on tour.

Having a name like Underwood has one disadvantage. It is almost at the bottom of the alphabet. And that means an agonizing wait for me whenever I turn on the radio or the television waiting for a Test team or a touring party to be announced.

Unless any changes are announced in the headlines it means I am one of the last to know whether I have been selected or omitted. Apart from the captain, the names of the other players are always listed in alphabetical order. I have to go through the entire rigmarole of 'Amiss, Boycott, d'Oliveira, Edrich, Fletcher, Greig . . .' So many names seem to be reeled off that there doesn't seem any space left to fit me in even when I am selected. It must be worse for Bob Willis and I'd hate to be a player with a surname starting with 'Z'.

I was on my way to play for Kent in a championship match at Dover with my brother Keith when I suffered one of my greatest disappointments in cricket. The party to tour the West Indies for the 1967–68 tour was being announced that day and I happened to pull into a garage for petrol when the news was due.

I was filling up when the party was named: 'Cowdrey, captain, Barrington, Boycott, etc'. On it went. I heard the name of Hobbs. Then came Pocock. Snow was next on the list followed by Titmus and I knew then I had missed the plane. Titmus made three spinners in the party. I knew there could not be room for any more.

It was the mention of Pocock's name which told me I had not been selected. Titmus was an obvious candidate and Hobbs was expected to go to use his leg-spinners on the West Indies wickets which should give him the bounce and pace he needed. The choice of the third spinner rested between Pocock, who had not played in a Test match at that stage of his career, and myself who had the grand total of four Test appearances against my name. With Pocock in I knew I was out. And I was heartbroken.

I'd had another good season at home and thought I stood a very good chance of making the final sixteen. I was feeling worse by the time I had parked my car at Dover and reached the dressing-room. On the way many Kent people had stopped me and said 'Hard luck'. Colin was waiting for me in the dressing-room. As captain he had been in on the selection committee.

He drew me to one side and told me, 'It might not be a bad thing from your point of view. The tour is probably too early for you. Never in the history of West Indies tours has a finger spinner done well out there. You are young yet and you will get another chance.' His words did not really help, but on reflection he was probably right.

We were playing Essex that day, and two lads who commiserated with me were Robin Hobbs and Keith Fletcher. Keith told me he had been approached to see whether he would like to go on a tour which Joe Lister, the present Yorkshire secretary, was hoping to arrange to East Africa, the Middle and the Far East. Mickey Stewart, the Surrey captain, was going to lead the tour.

Later that day I approached Colin and told him I would like to get on a tour that winter to gain experience of bowling on hard and fast wickets. I mentioned the proposed Lister tour. He immediately phoned Lister and a fortnight later came a letter asking me if I was available. I jumped at the opportunity and it proved one of the highlights of my cricketing career.

I didn't quite get the hard wicket experience I was looking for. Wherever we went rain seemed to have preceded us, and I had any number of wet wickets on which to bowl. I finished the three month tour by taking a stack of wickets, although only a quarter of them were first class. But the experience of being on a tour, being away from home for three months, and living with a crowd of players day in and day out proved invaluable.

The importance of this was brought home to me quite recently, when David Lloyd, the Lancashire captain and the discovery of the 1974 summer, was chatting to me as we stood on the balcony before a pre-Test match dinner.

I glanced up at a block of flats overlooking the Lord's ground, and commented to David, 'It wouldn't be bad living on one of the higher floors so that you could sit on the balcony and watch cricket.'

He followed my gaze and said, 'Not for me. I don't like heights.'

'You had better get used to them,' I told him. 'You'll be going much higher than that when you fly around Australia this winter.'

It was then that he surprised me. 'I've never been in a plane,' he answered.

Flying around the world had become part and parcel of my cricketing life, and it seemed incredible that a fellow cricketer had never flown. Thinking about it more seriously it was not so surprising. But for cricket I too might never have been in a plane. I then realized what David was taking on. He was entering an entirely different kind of life on tour.

This conversation made me realize how fortunate I had been to cut my touring teeth with Joe Lister. The longest I had been away from home before then was with the MCC Under-25 side to Pakistan, and that had been only six weeks.

With Joe Lister I learned what it was like bowling long spells in hot and humid conditions even though I did not encounter too many hard wickets. And I learned a lot about life and people. In the majority of places we visited we stayed privately. There were many others with me who now form the nucleus of the England side including Denness, Greig, Fletcher and Amiss.

We visited Sierra Leone, Uganda, Pakistan, India, Ceylon, Singapore, Bangkok, Malacca and Kuala Lumpur among other places, and finished up in Hong Kong. A wonderful experience for a twenty-three-year-old. I met some great characters as well, including a batsman in Sierra Leone whose name was Ponsford Benka-Coker. Unbelievably, he had a brother called Bradman Benka-Coker.

Wickets were quite cheap, especially in the places where it had rained, or on the matting wickets. I remember taking seven for 30 against a Singapore XI, eight for 19 at Seremban on matting, and eleven for 40 in a match in Kuala Lumpur.

I also returned from that tour with a remarkable analysis

which earned a line in Wisden. That happened in a three day match against the Ceylon President's XI in Colombo on a wet wicket. I emerged from their first innings with figures of 11.3-6-10-8. I followed that up in their second innings by taking seven for 33 in our 194 run win. The President's XI were dismissed for 42 and 98.

Perhaps the most satisfying performance was in Madras against the Chief Minister's XI, another first class three day match. I had been left out of the games in Karachi and Bombay, so this was my first experience of hard wickets since that Under-25 tour to Pakistan. We won by 290 runs. I took six for 41 in the first innings, and three for 12 in the second, against some of India's leading batsmen, including a fair sprinkling of Test players. Those were the two first class games in which I played on the tour, bagging me twenty-four wickets at four runs apiece. A nice little boost to my career record.

The match in Karachi produced one surprising incident. The pitch had started to break up on the second day, and when we arrived for the last day with the opposition due to bat to save the match, we found that all the holes and marks had been filled in. Not only filled in, but watered down and rolled. Quite rightly Mickey Stewart refused to play until all the holes had been put back in the wicket and he threatened to report the Pakistan authorities to Lord's. The holes were duly replaced and we won the match.

I've heard several of the older players in the game say that Stewart would have made a good England captain if he had been a little more consistent with the bat, and I must say I was impressed with the way he handled the side on the tour. It was hard to maintain a keen, professional approach against some of the opposition we met in the one day and two day fixtures, but Mickey kept everybody on their toes and insisted on full net practice, even though we did not need to be at our best to overcome some sides.

I did have one disappointment on that tour. Before I had left England, MCC had asked me to be a stand-by replacement should any injuries arise on the MCC tour in the West Indies. We were in Bombay when we heard the news that Fred Titmus has lost four toes in a boating accident just off Barbados and would not be taking any further part in the tour. As the stand-by spinner I was getting ready to fly to the Caribbean when the news came that they had sent for Tony Lock instead. He had just ended another impressive season with his left-arm spinners for Western Australia and taken them to the Sheffield Shield title as captain.

There is no doubt that playing on tour does not contain the same pressures as playing at home. Overseas I can be ticking over getting my one for 30, two for 40, etc, while waiting for my opportunity. It does become agonizing though if you play in only two matches in a fortnight – as can happen if you miss out on a Test match – and fail to get a wicket in that time.

On the other hand, if I were at home taking one for 30 and two for 40 I would be worried. On tour I might be the only left-arm spinner in the party, so if one was required for a particular match or wicket they would have no alternative but to select me. But at home the selectors would have five or six others from which to choose. So if I didn't contribute then I'd know I would be likely to be out.

I know I have been very nervous playing for MCC against the touring side at Lord's, especially if my bowling has been criticized the previous summer or during a winter away. I'm sure these matches are looked on as trial games.

At Lord's I am usually bowling from the nursery end because of the slope from the Father Time Grandstand to the Tavern. The slope helps the ball move away from the right-handed batsman if the wicket is offering a little. It can be most disheartening before starting my run to glance up and see the four England selectors huddled in a group high up on the dining-room balcony, studying the scene intently.

If I did toss one up, and force the batsman to use his feet and play defensively, I used to think to myself, 'Did they see that one? Were they impressed?' Of course if I attempt a slower ball and the batsman slams it out of sight then I'm hoping the attention of the selectors has been distracted for that moment, and they didn't see what had happened.

After visiting all the major Test playing countries apart from South Africa, and sampling life in a few others, I must admit that Pakistan is not one of my favourites. My view has nothing to do with the country itself, or the people. It is just that I have found the wicket conditions the hardest to bowl on in my career.

And my last two visits have coincided with moments of political unrest.

At least in India the ball just stops and holds a little, as it can do in England. That is all I ask for, although they also have a number of 'nothing wickets' – slow, low tracks with no bounce. Yet touring those two countries can be the most pleasant of trips. I found the team spirit on the 1972–73 tour to India and Pakistan under Tony Lewis the best I have encountered, and that counts for a great deal.

There is so little to do in the evenings, so little to see and visit that the whole party must stick together and make its own fun if the trip is to be a success.

The conditions in some of the up-country places were poor, but we all enjoyed ourselves in the end, meeting each night in the largest room available for the odd beer or two – when we could get it – swapping jokes and stories. But the going was tough at times.

In the other countries there is so much to see and do that the spirit is not quite the same. On days off or in the evenings the tour party is usually split up into three, four, or even five sections, and is only really together when playing or travelling between each centre. A real team spirit is essential overseas, and this stems, of course, from smooth running, the relationship between the captain and manager, and success on the field.

There is one aspect of touring which annoys me, and one I believe the Test and County Cricket Board have got to change in the near future. That is the insistence of trying to turn professional cricketers into touring ambassadors. Such an attitude might have been all right thirty or forty years ago, when we were trying to introduce cricket to other countries and improve the standing of the game overseas. When England was the best side in the world. Now these other countries are on a par with us. They have grown up.

There is nothing more annoying on tour than having to go to social functions and attend rounds of parties listening to social chit-chat which doesn't concern us. We have many such official functions, and they are supposed to stop when Test matches are in progress. That is the rule but it has often been broken. The team does not go anywhere as a large party during Test matches, but successive managers often detail 'volunteers' to represent the tour party at dinners and even private house parties.

This, I believe, is wrong to a certain extent. More often than not people send in these invitations because they want to impress their friends and not because they are really interested in us, as players or people. Everywhere we go we have to attend functions organized by Government bodies. Quite frankly, these are usually a great bore. They often put on a reception for us because they feel it is their duty.

I would much sooner slip off to the local cricket club or somewhere like that. To be among people who really want to meet us and who want to discover more about cricket. This would spread the gospel of cricket far better than attending all the official receptions. And no cricketer should ever be asked to go out during a Test match if he does not want to.

Another trend crept in during the MCC tour of the West Indies in 1973–74 when we were ordered to share a drink with the opposing team at the end of each day of the Test matches. We were expected to go into their dressing-room or have them in ours. I think this was wrong.

I know why such orders were made. It was hoped that such a move would ease any tensions which might have developed on the field, and bring a quick end to any feeling which might have crept into the game. But I don't think any player should have to drink with members of the opposition if he doesn't want to. Some players like sharing a beer afterwards. That's perfectly all right. The Australians often came into our dressing-room and we visited their room, but it should be left to the individual.

Personally it is not my scene. Once I've come off the field I like to get away from the ground as quickly as possible, get back to my hotel room and unwind in a quiet, relaxed atmosphere. Once I've done that I'm all for sharing a beer if any member of the opposition is around. I don't want to have a drink just for the sake of having a drink, especially with somebody who might have tried to knock my head off with a bouncer a few minutes before or who had taken toll of my bowling. Several times in the West Indies I found myself sitting between two West Indian players talking excitedly to each other. When they do that, difficulties of interpretation arise. Go into the Indian or Pakistani dressing-room and many of their players are talking to each other in their own language. I have often felt awkward sitting there with a beer in my hand, unable to understand what is being said.

The tour to Pakistan in 1969 did give me my biggest surprise on an overseas tour. While the authorities rearranged the tour because of the riots we went off on a three match tour of up-country districts. One stage of this tour meant a late coach journey across a desert area. All our luggage was piled on top of a van and sent on early. A couple of English cricket writers went with this van, partly to help look after the luggage and partly in the hope of claiming the best rooms left in the next hotel outside those allotted to the team.

Their plan misfired when the van broke down in the middle of the desert. The lights failed and the driver could not see a thing. This was dangerous when so many other vehicles on the road did not have lights either, and it was often littered with families driving their small herds of cattle ahead of them.

The two journalists abandoned the truck and we found them in the middle of the road out in the desert desperately waving us down. They were worried that we might have sneaked ahead by a different route out of town and were most relieved to see our coach. The luggage van was left to limp along later, and when we went to collect our luggage the next morning mine was missing. All my cricket gear and spare clothes were inside.

I said goodbye to my gear and was making arrangements to cable for replacements from London when they turned up. Some chap with a cart and oxen had found my case lying in a ditch by the side of the road across the desert, recognized the initials MCC, and handed them in. I'd never expected to see any of that gear again.

9. ON THE RECEIVING END

Night watchman extraordinary . . . Bouncers and tail-enders . . . The wrath of the fast bowler . . . A record partnership with Amiss at Sabina Park.

For a cricketer who realized fairly early in his first class career that his bat was not the most essential item of his equipment, I've found myself being required to pad up at the same time as some of the finest opening batsmen in the world.

If England are to start an innings any time in the last hour of the day it has become automatic now that I start strapping on my pads alongside Boycott and Amiss or whoever else is going in number one or two. Somehow or other I've joined the mug's game of becoming England's recognized night watchman. How and when it started I've no idea. But I can only guess that it must have begun with Kent under Colin Cowdrey. When Colin was captaining England and needed a night watchman he automatically turned to me. I certainly never asked for the job, but it seems to have stuck.

The only time I can't remember having to do it was in Australia when Ray Illingworth asked Knott to go in. Ray didn't want to lose another senior batsman that night but we didn't have much time to spare, and Knotty going in would make sure the runs were scored at a fairly healthy rate the next morning.

Perhaps my first Test innings helped get me the role, when d'Oliveira and I put on those 65 runs for the final wicket against the West Indies at Trent Bridge. I've played a part – a very lucky one at times – in four or five late partnerships which have helped to put on valuable runs. Mostly my role has been to stay there, leaving the scoring to the senior batsman. That is all a night watchman is required to do – stay there.

Once I even managed to take over the scoring role as well in a Test match. That was against the Australians at Headingley in 1968, when David Brown and I teamed up for the final wicket after nine wickets had gone down in our first innings for 241.

This was on a wicket which was helping the spinners one end. Faced with the prospect of batting last we wanted to get as near to the Australian first innings total as possible, but all hope appeared lost when the ninth wicket fell at 241 in reply to Australia's 315. Alan Connolly had been the Australian dangerman, bowling his cutters from the rugby stand end and moving the ball quite sharply off the pitch at times.

In those circumstances it didn't seem likely that either David or I would stay around long. This time it wasn't a question of me trying to stay there while a recognized batsman scored runs from the other end, so I thought that if my stay was going to be short it might as well be as profitable as I could make it.

There was another reason why I started swinging. When I first went in Barry Jarman, leading Australia in the absence of the injured Bill Lawry, crowded nine fielders around the bat. I hate that. It makes me nervous. So I decided I must try and make a few retreat or else I would not have any chance of staying long. They crowded me, I knew, because I came in on a hat-trick.

The wide open spaces beyond the close ring looked inviting, especially on the leg side where most of my elegant cross-batted shots seem to put the ball, and I started swinging. It brought me 45 runs – my best Test score up to the end of the 1974 summer – in fifty-three minutes, and David and I added 61.

More than half those runs came against Connolly, who had figures of five for 41 when I went in and finished up with five for 72 by the time Cowper bowled Brown with his off-spinners. To be fair to Connolly, he had bowled almost thirty overs by the time I arrived at the crease and was almost on his knees. But the important fact was that we managed to take England's score to within 13 runs of the Australian first innings total, which proved helpful when we started out to save the match on the final day.

Going in as a night watchman has resulted in me having to deal with far more bouncers than a normal number ten or eleven batsman expects to receive in his cricketing lifetime.

The question of a fast bowler hurtling down bouncers at tail-enders has caused controversy in all parts of the world. Most people would argue that it just isn't done. A tail-ender is not equipped to deal with bouncers technically as a batsman, and it is asking for a player to be hit and seriously injured from a blow on the head. But the odd one or two are acceptable if the tail-ender has managed to stay around for some time and he's shown he is seeing the ball quite well.

So the bowling of bouncers to nine, ten, jack is considered taboo, yet few people raise serious objections if a night watchman gets a few. Apparently it is not the standard of the batsman which gives the go-ahead to the bowling of bouncers, but the position he bats. Don't bowl bouncers at a number ten batsman. But if that number ten batsman goes in at number three or four in an emergency it is all right. I've never understood that argument.

As I said earlier, I've had to put up with an unfair number of them at times in my night watchman role, when the new ball bowlers have been fresh and striving for another wicket before the close. Strangely I've not been hit in those circumstances – at the time of writing – but have taken a few blows when batting in my normal position.

The first time caused a considerable rumpus. It was in my first Test match and the 'villain' was none other than Charlie Griffith. He sent me sprawling all over the pitch. And I was lucky. I might easily have ended up in a Nottingham hospital that night.

It was absolutely uncalled for. That was the staggering part about the delivery – plus some doubt about its authenticity.

It happened in the England second innings as the West Indies were cruising to victory. They had declared on the fourth afternoon, setting us 393 to win in seven hours. After being 30 without loss overnight our hopes were dashed on that last morning by the combination of Hall and Griffith.

Colin Milburn was out almost immediately on the last morning when caught attempting to hook against Hall, and any thought of winning was scuttled when Russell, Graveney and Parks fell cheaply. Any thought of survival disappeared when Boycott's brave innings of 71 was ended with a fine slip catch by Sobers, who also accounted for Cowdrey in the same position. When d'Oliveira left with two hours to go, a West Indies victory was not far away.

Now only the tail was left, and that's why I thought the Griffith bouncer was entirely out of place. I was last man and had newly arrived at the wicket to partner Snow when he unleashed it. Admittedly I had stayed around for 85 minutes in the first innings with Dolly, but the chance of a repeat performance was out of the question.

I never saw the ball until a fraction of a second before I was hit. One second Griffith was holding it as he went into his delivery stride. The next it was rearing towards my face. I just managed to get my glove up, taking the pace off the ball before it glanced into my face and down I went. I was pretty dazed for a few moments. I gather the West Indies players rushed over to help me to my feet – except Charlie. He had turned his back on the whole scene and was strolling back to his mark.

Snow, too, rushed down the wicket to assist me and helped break the atmosphere when a glass of water was brought out for me to drink. 'Whatever you do, don't spit it out on a length,' he said. He has a crack for most occasions.

Gary, so I was told later, did rebuke Charlie on the field before my legs had stopped shaking sufficiently to hold the weight of my body again. Time and time again, Griffith would let one go on the last ball of the over and this was the last ball I ever faced from him. Later that evening he told the cricket writers: 'I just don't think it is right to bowl bouncers to tail-enders.'

Actually that was rather strange coming from Gary at that time. He had bowled me quite a vicious bouncer in the first innings, which hurt almost as much as the one from Griffith. It caught me on the left arm.

That was done in a fit of temper. Dolly had gone for a quick single in an attempt to take the next over, and the West Indies players – Gary in particular – were convinced they had run me out when a direct throw broke the wicket. He was very upset when I was given not out, and was probably entitled to be. It was a close thing. So the next time that I faced Gary he bowled me that bouncer as if I was responsible for still being at the wicket. But you can't argue with the umpire over a run out.

There had been no incident to provoke the one from Griffith, and the reaction of most experts on the ground was that the delivery was a Griffith 'special'. Earlier that afternoon he had bowled one against Cowdrey which came near to crowning Colin as it whizzed through. Colin is a magnificent hooker of the ball, one of the best players against fast bowling the game has produced in the last twenty years, but he had no chance to react against that delivery.

The incident had a sequel four days later when Kent played the West Indies at Canterbury. I was playing for Kent, but Charlie had been rested from the West Indies side and I gather the decision was taken after the Trent Bridge bouncer. He had been down to play originally.

Before the match started I went into the toilet and was followed in by Jeff Stollmeyer, the former Trinidad and West Indies opening batsman and selector who was managing the 1966 West Indies tour party. There were just the two of us in there and he gave me an envelope before turning on his heels and going out. It was a letter from Charlie and I still have it at home among my cricket souvenirs.

The envelope and letter paper were inscribed 'The West Indies Cricket Tour of England 1966', and my name had been scrawled across the front. The letter was dated that day and read:

> Dear Derek, I would like you to know that I am sorry you received that blow at Trent Bridge. I assure you there was nothing deliberate about the delivery and am glad to hear that the injury is not serious. Yours sincerely, Charlie.

It was a charming little letter, but I thought Charlie might have apologized to me personally. And that Stollmeyer might have chosen a better place than the toilet at Canterbury to hand me the letter if Charlie couldn't bring himself to give it to me personally.

On another occasion I was the object of a series of bouncers which I thought were uncalled for. This time it was Mike Procter in a Kent v. Gloucestershire match at Tunbridge Wells. They came out of the blue and were delivered in a fit of temper, although I had not been the cause of Procter's annoyance. The crowd had irritated him when some spectators had made rude remarks about Gloucestershire's slow over rate, and Procter's long walk back to his mark. They upset him, but it was me he took it out on with his bouncers. I didn't improve his temper either. The pitch was so slow that even I had time to shovel the ball round behind square leg. This prompted him to have another go at me. Fortunately for my state of health it was a verbal blistering and not more bouncers.

The most bouncers I have ever faced in my role as night

watchman came in February 1974 when we were trying to save the second Test against the West Indies in Jamaica. And I was most grateful for them!

After the West Indies had answered our first innings 353 by scoring 583 for nine declared – Lawrence Rowe making his customary century on his home ground of Sabina Park, Kingston – we were in desperate trouble the second time round. Shortly before the close of play on the fourth day our fifth wicket, that of Greig, fell with the score at 217.

Boycott, Jameson, Hayes, Denness and Greig were all back in the pavilion, and of our specialist batsmen only Amiss was still surviving, struggling on against fierce West Indian pressure and displaying the temperament and character of which great players are made. Of our 217 runs he had made 123, but we were still 13 runs short of making the West Indies bat again.

That was the situation when Mike Denness sent me out that evening to keep our last remaining batting hope, Knott, free for the last day. After Knott there were only Chris Old, Pat Pocock and Bob Willis to come.

I shall never forget arriving in the middle where Amiss was ready to greet me. He surprised me by saying: 'You're not out here just to protect Knotty, you know. You're here to protect me as well.' I found this difficult to understand. He was 123 not out at the time.

There were still some fifteen minutes to go, and I suppose he was right. Although he had been at the wicket four hours and was seeing the ball clearly, he was obviously very tired after being out in the hot Jamaican sun all day. I think I did take more of the bowling in those final fifteen minutes. I know I scored the only run added in that time.

But back to the question of bouncers and what I think about them. I didn't fancy going to the wicket that night because Kanhai had Gibbs bowling his off-spinners from one end, with the local leg-spinning hero Arthur Barrett at the other. As soon as Kanhai saw me, he doubled his ring of fielders around the bat. They were so close there was hardly room for the ball to get through.

This time there was no question of me having a swing in an attempt to scatter them. I couldn't risk making a mistake. I just had to stay there, get on the front foot and block it out. I hated it.

In fact I think I was out that night. When facing Barrett I'm sure I got a little nick against one delivery. I felt the bat move a little as I played at the ball and it carried through to the wicket-keeper. But nobody appealed. The umpire was never called upon to make a decision and I didn't have to make up my mind whether I should have to walk.

I wasn't looking forward to going back again on that final morning, because the new ball was seven overs away and I knew I would be facing the spinners again at the start. So it proved. Somehow I managed to keep the ball out of my wicket and away from clutching hands, and I was quite relieved when I saw Kanhai call up Boyce and Julien to take the new ball. Even though I knew I was going to get a few bouncers.

Boyce did not let me down. He was slipping two or three short pitched balls an over. Nothing was said by the umpires. They took the view that the wicket was so good and yet so slow that the short pitched deliveries were not dangerous enough to justify a warning for intimidation. They had a point. It must have been the easiest batting strip on which I have ever played.

Certainly that final day brought a unique experience for me in my night watchman duties. I lasted long enough to still be at the crease when the first drinks interval was due after forty minutes' play. And I almost made it to the next drinks interval as well but Sobers, bowling a quicker ball, drifted it away and I couldn't get my bat out of the way quickly enough to avoid giving a catch behind.

In an effort to give me confidence Amiss walked down the wicket to me after one battering from Boyce and said, 'Stick with it Deadly. You're playing the bouncers better than I am.'

'I have to play them,' I told him. 'I can see them coming but I'm not good enough to get out of the way.'

Really that just about sums it up. Whenever I see a bouncer coming I automatically get into line, body behind the bat and ball. That was what I was brought up to do. Nobody ever told me what I should do next and I've never learned. That is why, when I play a bouncer, I can usually be seen with the shoulder of my bat tucked under my chin and both feet nine inches off the ground trying to get above the ball and keep it down. It is not often I succeed, the ball glancing off the bat at all angles. The boys often pull my leg over this.

I've never learned to sway out of the way as Greig does, or duck, which is Knott's method of avoiding them. I think Knotty is a marvel in the way he avoids the ball, letting it fly harmlessly through well above him. He is not the slightest bit ruffled. He just squats down on his haunches as though he is going to go into one of his now familiar exercise routines. More like a Cossack dancer getting ready to give a display.

That last day at Sabina Park was a nerve-tingling time as Knott followed me but soon became a run out victim. Fortunately Old lasted out 110 minutes and Pocock another 85. Even when last man Willis went in there would still have been an outside chance of a West Indies victory if he had got out within five minutes, but he played his part as well. Amiss was absolutely superb. How he summoned up the strength to last there throughout the final day in making his 262 not out I shall never know. He was almost out on his feet he was so exhausted, but that bat never wavered as it came down to meet the ball square on. His was one of the greatest match saving innings in the history of the game, and I shall count myself fortunate to have seen it.

The subject of bouncers on that tour recalls one funny incident in the final Test involving Keith Fletcher. The story began after the Jamaican Test. At a reception that evening Fletcher was having a good-natured go at his Essex colleague Boyce about the bouncers.

'It's a good job I wasn't playing,' he told him. 'I'd have smashed you all round the ground.' Fletcher had missed that Test because of illness.

Not to be outdone Boyce replied, 'If I bowled bouncers at you, you'd never survive. They would be too fast for you, man.'

'Just you wait and see,' said Fletcher. 'You're not good enough or fast enough to hit me with a bouncer.'

These two finally came face to face in the final Test at Port of Spain, Trinidad. Boyce had missed the third Test in Barbados – where Greig saved us with a century in the first innings and Fletcher denied West Indies a victory with a century in our second innings – and the fourth Test was rained off before they could face each other.

When Boyce found himself with the ball in his hand and Fletcher in his sights in Trinidad he did let him have a bouncer. Not one but several. So many that in the end Fletcher walked up the wicket to umpire Douglas Sang Hue and asked him, 'How do you interpret the intimidation rule out here then, umpire?'

'They are not bouncers,' replied Sang Hue. 'They are only long-hops.'

'Funny long-hops that whistle past yer ear'ole,' remarked Fletcher as he walked back to the crease – and faced more bouncers.

Fletcher is only a little guy, not much bigger than Knott. A quiet chap as well, off the field, but he has bags of determination and speaks up for himself when he has to.

I remember another occasion on which Fletcher walked the length of the wicket to make a protest. That was on the MCC Under-25 tour in Pakistan during a match against the Board of Control Eleven in Rawalpindi, the one wicket in Pakistan where the ball does turn.

Saeed Ahmed, the Pakistan off-spinner and batsman leading the Board of Control side, was eager to make an impression so as to improve his chances of taking control of the full Pakistan Test side. Saeed, on the field, often gets carried away by his enthusiasm when appealing, and attempts to pressurize umpires. We had already had one brush with him on that tour when he ran out Geoff Arnold as he was backing up. He did it without any warning when Geoff, having tucked into Saeed quite healthily, was 73.

At Rawalpindi Saeed was appealing for practically everything: for leg-before decisions, for catches when the ball had clearly struck only the pad, for nicks behind off the body. He made one such appeal against Fletcher and almost went frantic when the umpire turned him down. Finally Fletcher could not stand it any more. In the middle of an over from Saeed he walked the length of the wicket and told him quietly, 'Why don't you cut out all this appealing and get on with playing the game properly. It would be better for everybody.'

It took a lot of courage for a twenty-two-year-old to say that to an established Test player ten years his senior. His protest worked as well.

Promotion up the order to night watchman resulted in me making my highest score in first class cricket when I scored exactly 80 against Lancashire at Old Trafford in 1969. It seems impossible, but that score is true. Not only did I make my top score in first class cricket but managed to be Kent's highest scorer in that match by no less than 43 runs.

We had been given the run around on the first day when David Bailey and Harry Pilling each scored centuries, sharing a stand of 255, and enabled Lancashire to declare on the first evening with their score 317 for six. There was not much time for Mike Denness and Brian Luckhurst to play out that evening, but Peter Lever struck for Lancashire by having Luckhurst caught. That was the signal for me to take over.

We were 17 for one overnight and 17 for two first thing next morning, when Higgs had Denness leg-before in his first over. I shall never forget Mike's face as he turned from the wicket to take his walk to the dressing-room. At that moment a church clock down the road struck 11.30. We'd actually started playing a couple of minutes before the official starting time!

With Lever, Higgs and Shuttleworth Lancashire had a more than useful attack, but I managed to last out until the afternoon session. How I did it I don't know. I suppose my performance is best summed up by a newspaper cutting I have kept which described my performance.

> The most significant innings for Kent was inescapably that of Underwood who stayed for three and a half hours and scored 80, which was 33 runs more than he had previously made in the first class game. To be truthful, he did not look notably a better batsman when he was out than when he went in but Lancashire could neither beat his defensive prod, nor hold the ball when he offered a chance, nor cut out his scoring shots.

I think the writer overdid it a little. His report makes me sound better than I can remember.

I thought I was going to have a chance of improving my highest Test score during the 1974 summer when I went in as night watchman against Pakistan at the Oval in the final game. We had nothing else to fight for but a draw after Pakistan made more than 600 in their first innings.

I had all the time in the world. We had no target, no time limit, when I went in. Our only aim was to survive as long as possible, with Fletcher doing it well in making one of the slowest Test centuries on record. I was eventually out for 43, two short of my Test best.

Earlier that summer at Old Trafford I had gone in as night watchman to join Fletcher against the Indians. Another innings I didn't particularly fancy, with Bedi bowling and the fielders all round the bat.

'How you feeling, Fletch?' I called out as I walked to the wicket.

'I'm all right,' he said. 'I've had my benefit!'

It was quite a tense and tight situation, but you would never have known it from him. He was enjoying himself.

I suppose I have been out as a night watchman, but I can't remember when. There is one person who is sure that I have failed at least once, and that's Chris Old. In doing some preparation for this book during that Pakistan Test at the Oval I remarked to Chilly that I couldn't remember being out when batting number three or four, but he remembers an occasion when he bowled me. I wouldn't argue with him. He's a quickie who is prepared to bowl bouncers at tail enders if the need arises!

10. CATCHES CAUGHT, CATCHES DROPPED

I drop it, and England loses! . . . A catch to be proud of . . . Doubtful decisions . . . Dolly drops a dolly . . . A non-catch to remember.

I don't think I would be out of place in claiming to have won a Test match here and there for England through my bowling. But on the other hand I must also admit to having blundered and denied England victory. Not through bowling but in the field, when I failed to hold on to a catch.

The occasion was at Headingley in 1974 in the first Test match against Pakistan, when I grassed a catch offered by Asif Masood in the Pakistan first innings. Asif is not the worst number eleven batsman in the world, but he would certainly admit he was far from the best. Normally a miss against him would not prove too expensive. This time it was disastrous.

Pakistan had been rather fortunate to reach 223 for nine by the time Asif Masood arrived at the crease. The wicket was a little awkward, but the atmospheric conditions were ideal for seam and swing bowling. Geoff Arnold, in particular, as well as Mike Hendrick and Chris Old used them superbly in beating the bat time and time again as the Pakistan batsmen were drawn forward. But they did not get the nicks and edges their bowling deserved. At times the ball was doing just a bit too much. Those conditions persisted every time the cloud level dropped, which was frequently over those five days.

There were just a few minutes to go on that first day when Asif Masood walked to the wicket to join Sarfraz Nawaz. They were not parted until an hour before lunch on the second day, by which time their partnership had grown to 62 – the highest of the innings. Thanks to yours truly.

In the last over of the day, with the score 226 for nine, Asif Masood drove loosely against Old. The ball came to me at cover – and down it went. The catch which cost England the match. Not only did I drop it, but Asif used the fumble to sneak a run and get off the mark. I did not realize at the time how expensive that miss was going to be.

In terms of runs Asif Masood did not profit much by the miss the following morning. He had made only another four by the time the Pakistan first innings closed. The batsman to make the most of it was Sarfraz, who made 53, his top score in Test cricket.

Sarfraz fancies himself as a batsman, and he showed exactly why that second morning with a number of handsome cover drives, standing up straight and really powering the ball through the field. He is a strange character. Roger Prideaux, then captaining Northants, had discovered him in a park in Lahore when he and Colin Cowdrey went for a net session during the 1969 tour of Pakistan. Roger was impressed and cabled Northants for permission to sign him to solve the county's fast bowling shortage. As soon as the Pakistan authorities heard of it they picked Sarfraz for the final Test of that tour.

At first Sarfraz didn't really settle down. After a couple of seasons Northants let him go, and Sarfraz went into League cricket in this country and turned himself into an all-rounder. This is partly the reason Northants took him back. He certainly looked in good form at Headingley.

Like the Griffith bouncer in my first Test match at Trent Bridge, I just didn't see the ball on that first evening until it was upon me. I watched the ball from Old's arm on to the bat and saw Asif make the stroke. I knew it was going to come in my direction. Then I lost sight of it completely against the dark background of the terraced seats opposite the pavilion. If I had been able to watch the ball all the way there is no doubt I would have had time to move into position and take the catch with both hands. When I did pick up the ball again it was going just to my right. I had hardly moved, stuck out my right hand and the ball hit the hard part just below the palm and popped out again. From 226 for nine, when the incident happened, the partnership grew to 285 by the time Pakistan were all out. Not until the fifth morning, when the ground was sodden, did I realize how important those extra runs were going to be.

Those awkward weather conditions persisted when we batted for the first time and were dismissed for 183, and the clouds were still low on the Saturday when Pakistan went in for a second time and were all out for 179. We started our final innings that Saturday evening needing 282 to win.

Take away the 59 runs the Pakistan last wicket pair had added after I dropped the catch and this target would have been reduced to 223. We had already scored more than that when the heavy overnight rain washed out the final day. That is why I say I must have cost England the match by my fielding blunder. Not only would England have won the match, but I'm sure we would have won the three match series.

The rain on the Monday evening was a tragedy, for it ruined what should have been a magnificent finish. With Edrich scoring 70 and Fletcher 67 not out England had scored 238 for six by the close on the Monday evening. We wanted another 44 runs to win, and Pakistan wanted another four wickets. It was still anybody's match.

I was very depressed when I realized how costly the miss had been. Especially because it happened in a summer when I took probably my finest catch in first class cricket. That was at Lord's during the second Test against India. It didn't really have a bearing on the result because India were booked for defeat anyway, but I was pleased nevertheless. Especially as I took it almost in front of the Tavern and would have been in for some stick if I had allowed it to slip through my fingers.

I was hidden away in my normal third man position, which meant being on the long leg boundary when a left-handed batsman was at the crease. With so many more short pitched deliveries being bowled in Test cricket these days, and more left-handed batsmen about, long leg has become an important position chasing after full-blooded hooks, top edges and misshooks. I'd already taken one that day when Wadekhar attempted to hook, but my best was against Solkar.

Actually he made contact with the ball quite well, and it went soaring into the air to my left. At one stage it looked as if it might carry for a six down in front of the England dressing-room, which is on the right-hand side of the Lord's pavilion. I was just a yard or so inside the boundary when I stuck out my left hand and managed to reach the ball, but it didn't stick.

The ball started to fall towards the ground, but so did I. In stretching for it I overbalanced, but the act of falling gave me a second chance to grab the ball at ankle height. I'm told it looked most dramatic, especially as I had started running the wrong way in the first place.

Taking catches like these has a strange effect on you. Drop a relatively simple catch and you don't feel anything but a touch of embarrassment. Yet when you take a difficult catch, especially one where the ball has been in the air some time, then you suffer a reaction, a feeling of great relief rather like the sensation you get when you have braked suddenly in a car to avoid an accident.

Strangely enough the catch I considered my best up until that moment was also against Solkar, and involved diving to my left. It was more of a nose-dive this time. In fact, if I had gone any lower my nose would have ploughed a neat furrow in the Oval turf. That happened on the final day of the last Test against India in their three match tour of 1971.

They had started their second innings needing 173 for victory, and the match was still evenly poised when Solkar came in with India 124 for four. He is an obstinate little batsman with a very sound temperament, and we didn't want him hanging around for long. He was playing himself in gently when he attempted to drive against me. He hit the ball firmly and not far off the ground but I dived full length at the end of my follow-through and the ball stuck. However, it wasn't enough to stop India getting the runs to gain their first Test victory on English soil.

I have written earlier that the catch I was most thankful for making was in my first Test match against the West Indies at Trent Bridge, when I caught Kanhai soon after I had marred my international debut my dropping their opening batsman Lashley. But a catch I really wanted to see taken was at Sydney during the fourth Test of the 1970–71 tour. Not so much from England's point of view, for we won that game easily enough by 299 runs. This was just a personal thing.

The catch was offered right at the end of the Australian first innings, when they were trying to get close to our 332. After being quite well placed with 180 for four at the start of the fourth morning they collapsed. I had taken three wickets that morning, to make my total four in the innings, when last man Alan Connolly arrived at the wicket, Australia still 100 runs behind.

I had my chance of adding Connolly's wicket to my list when he took a swing at me but did not connect properly. The ball went up in the air to deep mid-on where d'Oliveira was standing underneath it. Unfortunately it went straight through his fingers.

Only twenty minutes or so before, Dolly had taken a fine running catch at deep square leg when Marsh had swept at me but hit it up in the air. The one from Connolly was much easier, perhaps too easy. And with the drop vanished my chance of taking five wickets in an innings in Australia, not only in Test matches but in all first class games. The nearest I got to it after that four wicket performance was a couple of times when I took three wickets in an innings.

Dolly and I had opened up with the bowling that morning, and we had done well enough for Ray Illingworth to delay taking the new ball. But when the catch went down Ray immediately summoned up Snow and Lever to blast out the final Australian resistance. Lever didn't let him down. As well as costing me my fifth wicket Dolly had also cost the Sydney authorities a new ball.

What do you say at a time like that? Nothing unless it is to offer a word of comfort. Nobody can catch them all. Sometimes they stick, sometimes they go down.

For instance, there was an occasion in the last championship match of the season against Surrey at the Oval in 1970, the year Kent won the title. The outcome had already been decided when the final day started, with us having gained sufficient bonus points on first innings to guarantee that Lancashire could not overhaul us. The match was petering out into a tame draw when I bowled one to Graham Roope, who is an extremely powerful driver of the ball. He just smashed at this one and hit it back in my direction, slightly to my left. It was four all the way, so Roope thought. It certainly seemed destined for the boundary until I instinctively thrust out my left hand and the ball nestled in it. It all happened so quickly I was surprised myself. Roope had hit the ball so hard I doubt whether I would have left my hand there if I realized what I was doing. He walked off the field shaking his head in amazement. Pity the catch didn't really mean anything.

One of the most amusing non-catches I can remember happened on the 1972–73 tour to India and Pakistan. This was during a match in Bombay when Greig was fielding in his silly point position, and I was bowling. For some unknown reason one delivery from me against the Nawab of Pataudi stopped and lifted, catching the top of his bat as he played forward. The ball shot up in the air and Greig had time to uncoil his 6ft 7in frame before it came down. My great grandmother could have caught it but the ball dropped straight through on to the deck. Poor Greig stood in horror and the rest of the boys could hardly restrain themselves from laughing when they looked at Greig's face.

The incident happened just before an interval, and as I walked off the field alongside our skipper Tony Lewis I remarked: 'That was cruel – cruel.'

Tony has never forgotten that remark. Every time he has written to me or met me since he greets me by saying 'That's cruel – cruel.'

11. KENT, A GREAT TEAM

The inspiration of Colin Cowdrey . . . Homegrown talent, and imported brilliance . . . Alan Knott, the best keeper of them all . . . Two teams I like to bowl against . . . My record – and the critics.

Over the years I have suffered a few setbacks and disappointments in my cricketing life. I've also got to admit that I have been extremely fortunate throughout most of my eleven seasons in the game up until the present time. My biggest stroke of fortune was joining Kent in the first place, not just because it is one of the best counties but because it happened at a particular time.

So often in life one man's misfortune means a completely unexpected chance for somebody else, and that happened in my case when David Halfyard was injured in a road accident late in the summer of 1962. His bad luck resulted in me being given my chance the following season, long before I had any right to consider a place in the first team.

In some ways it might have been better if I had spent another couple of seasons in the second team, playing in club and ground matches and learning the trade. I might then have been able to change my action and become the slower type of left-arm spinner so many people apparently want to see.

But I did have this early chance when I was still a seventeen-year-old, and did well enough to stay in the side. It meant that I got in on the ground floor just as the Kent side was beginning to be rebuilt. That process continued throughout the next four or five seasons.

Just about the same time as I got into the side Brian Luckhurst and Mike Denness were starting to establish themselves as first team players, beginning in the Kent middle order and progressing until they took over as the regular opening pair. Not long after me came another player who was to play a leading part in helping me reach the top – Alan Knott, the greatest little wicketkeeper I have seen and one who lives up to Kent's lofty standards in that department.

Norman Graham arrived about the same period as Knotty. Then John Shepherd and Asif Iqbal, followed by Bernard Julien in 1970. Before Bernard arrived the staff was building up with Alan Ealham, Bob Woolmer, Graham Johnson – two years behind me at Beckenham and Penge Grammar School – and the others.

I can't think of another county side which has had such a wealth of talent joining its ranks over the last 10 years. Happily the stream does not appear to have ended, thanks to the work of Colin Page with the second team. Colin has now taken over from Les Ames as cricket manager.

During all the celebrations which flowed in after we won the county championship in our centenary year of 1970, one important fact was overlooked outside the county border. That year the second eleven, captained by Colin Page, secured the double by winning the second eleven championship. That was a tremendous feat considering the serious calls made on second eleven players to fill first team places when Test calls disrupted the championship side.

All of us who arrived at Kent during that period were fortunate in another way – we had Colin Cowdrey leading the first team. He was a player who commanded respect by his performances on the field, and earned it by the way he treated us and his infectious enthusiasm. He was never too busy to listen, help and advise us. In a previous chapter I detailed some of the finest innings I've seen without mentioning one by Colin. I found that impossible. I saw so many. His long innings were all of such a high standard. He rarely tore into an attack like Sobers, Lloyd and others, but quietly assassinated the opposition with the perfection of his timing and placing of his shots. Poetry in motion, as they say.

Two of Colin's centuries particularly pleased me, not so much for their content but because they were landmarks which told of his greatness. The first was at Edgbaston against Australia in 1968 when he made his 100th Test appearance – the first player to do so – and celebrated with his twenty-first Test century. That one took courage and character, for he pulled a leg muscle before he reached 50 and his second half century was made almost on one leg without the aid of quick singles. He certainly deserved that one. As he did the one at Maidstone against Surrey in 1973 which brought him his 100th century, although he was batting at number seven. It was one of his fastest too, taking 140 minutes during which he outscored Asif. I was away playing for England at the time, but I raised my glass to him that night.

Behind Colin was Les Ames, a popular and genial man, but hard when it came to cricket. He has given me a lot of encouragement over the years but never too much praise. If Les says 'Well done', I know I must have bowled well.

He has never believed in kidding anybody along, and has always made sure that we take a realistic approach instead of drifting off into a dream world. In 1966, when I was selected for the Under-25 tour of Pakistan – of which he was manager – he wrote congratulating me on my selection, but in the same letter he warned me that I must not be too disappointed if I found the conditions hard and did not finish up with many wickets on the tour. In some ways the letter was a bit discouraging, but it also showed what a sound judge of a cricketer Les is. The tour went exactly as he expected as far as my bowling was concerned.

One of the most impressive features about Kent cricket over the last five seasons or so has been the way the county has managed to take so many honours and titles when the side has been so disrupted by Test calls. Not only has England claimed Luckhurst, Denness, Cowdrey, Knott and myself, but the West Indies took Julien in 1973 and Shepherd in 1969, and Pakistan called on Asif in 1967, 1971 and 1974.

Not only has the county's fine run spoken volumes for the strength and quality of the younger players waiting in the wings, but it has been a credit to the way the non-Test players have carried the extra burden heaped on their shoulders and have accepted being thrust up and down the batting order.

One moment Shepherd has found himself batting at three or four, only to be dropped down to seven or eight for the next match. It has happened to Knott who must have filled every batting position for Kent over the years, and again to Woolmer. And there has been David Nicholls jumping in and out of the side as Knotty's cover. It says a lot for the spirit of the side that these movements have taken place without a major row flaring up inside the camp. I can't think of many county sides where it would have been so peaceful in such circumstances.

In the gradual changeover in the late 1960s, and the rebuilding of the side, the one player we have not replaced adequately has been Alan Dixon whose great strength was in being able to bowl seamers and off-spinners. The lack of a specialist off-spinner is still a weakness, but one which I think could be solved quite easily.

When Mike Denness became Cowdrey's understudy and began to step down from his regular opening batting role, the county pushed Graham Johnson in as Luckhurst's opening partner. There Graham has stayed. He has done well, but I think the county could have used his ability better. I believe he has the potential to become a very good off-spin bowler, and I would much rather see him given a chance to exploit that ability by giving him more chance to bowl and not concentrating so much on his batting.

In my opinion he would be much better off going in at number seven where he would still have a chance of making his runs, free from the burden of opening the innings. He is such a natural hitter of the ball. This would also improve his chances of being selected for England. What an advantage he would be to the middle order: an off-spinner who is also a genuine batsman.

That would leave the opening batting position of Kent to be settled, and I still think that the combination of Denness and Luckhurst is the best one. But if Mike feels it is better for him to go in at number three from the captaincy point of view then I would like to see Woolmer given a chance as Luckhurst's partner. Bob is a sound player who has never really had a chance to show his true batting form for the county. And he is also a fine player of quick bowling.

Luckhurst has been an absolute marvel for Kent, and the way he has adapted himself to limited over cricket has been a credit to him. He is not a natural fast-scoring batsman, nor as attractive to watch as Denness. When they batted together it was the tortoise and the hare all over again. Nine times out of ten Mike would streak away in front when it came to scoring runs, but when it came to scoring centuries Luckhurst was much in evidence. It took Luckhurst a little time to match the requirements of limited over cricket, but during the last four seasons he has become one of the most imaginative batsmen in this type of cricket in the country. Some people still criticize his slowness off the mark, but I have always felt that with Luckhurst at the wicket we were in with a chance whatever the total and run rate required. He has not often let us down.

Although it was a great tragedy when Geoff Boycott announced he did not feel able to go on the 1974–75 Australian tour in defence of the Ashes, I was delighted when Luckhurst was named as his replacement. I thought he was the unluckiest batsman in the world when he was dropped from the England side in 1972, and then missed the MCC tour to India and Pakistan the following winter. He would have been a success out there. And in the West Indies the following winter. He is one of the most courageous batsmen I know.

One acquisition who has boosted Kent's batting, particularly in limited-over cricket, has been Asif Iqbal. He really enjoys his game and goes out into the middle with one objective in mind – to hit the ball. He is a fine player of spin bowling, using his feet well and refusing to become bogged down. He looks to score one four every over. If I were a batsman I would like to think I had his approach to the game. We've had some tremendous struggles over the years, generally with him coming out on top. He has been known to smash me all around the park in pre-season net sessions at Canterbury.

The spectators who were at the Oval for the final England Test against Pakistan in 1967 will surely never forget Asif's performance in the Pakistan second innings, when he made 146 batting at number eight. There seemed no way Pakistan could avoid defeat by an innings when Asif's turn came. They needed 224 to avoid an innings defeat when they started their second innings, were 53 for seven when Asif's innings started, and soon became 65 for eight before he found a partner in Intikhab. Together they put on 190 for the ninth wicket to set a new record in Test cricket.

Asif was devastating, and I was one of the bowlers to suffer. He didn't build an innings, but launched himself into the attack like a jet fighter being catapulted off an aircraft carrier. He raced to his 50 out of 56, excelling in the hook and the drive. Intikhab's share of the 100 partnership was 28.

Brian Close, captaining England for the last time, had maintained an attacking field at the start of Asif's innings, but there was no slackening in the scoring rate even when Close was forced to spread his men. Asif reached his century in only two hours 19 minutes with his 14th four, and we didn't see him again for almost five minutes. He was completely engulfed by the delighted Pakistan supporters who flocked all over the Oval wicket. He needed a drink to revive after all the back slappings and bruising hugs which he got then.

He had been at the wicket just over three hours for his 142 when, in desperation, Close decided to bowl himself and drew Asif out of his crease to leave Knott with a smart stumping. Intikhab was out in the next over for 51 but they had taken the Pakistan score from a humiliating 65 for eight to 255 all out, reducing England's margin of victory from a likely innings win to one by eight wickets.

Asif staggered everybody at the Oval that day except Dennis Amiss, Geoff Arnold, Knott and myself. We had seen him put on a similar display before when he was leading the Pakistan Under-25 team against us. That was the start of the trail which led him to Kent, for Les Ames had also witnessed that innings in Dacca.

Once again Asif's side was in a terrible position. Mike Brearley and Dennis Amiss had led the MCC Under-25 recovery with a partnership of 356 for the second wicket after we had seen Knott, opening in an emergency after Warwickshire's Neal Abberley had been sent home with a broken thumb, caught in the slips off Niaz without a run on the board. Niaz was a remarkable figure and rather a mystery as far as Test cricket was concerned. He was the only player of East Pakistan with any Test potential, but not really good enough to make the full Pakistan team. Yet he was always sure of earning a Test cap. Whenever a Test was played in Dacca, then the capital of East Pakistan, Niaz was the first to be chosen and the other ten players pencilled in afterwards. It would have been unthinkable – and dangerous – to have played a Test in Dacca without the local hero in the side. Imagine the delight when he claimed Knott's wicket in his first over.

Brearley and Amiss shrugged off the setback. Brearley was in sparkling form, following his 300 in one day a fortnight earlier by making 223 in just over six and a half hours. Amiss was less sure, being dropped four times, but he soldiered on to score 131.

Even when these two were out the runs still kept flowing. Fletcher chipped in with a bright 72 before the last six wickets went down for 64 against the slow left arm bowling of Pervez. We still reached 475.

The spin combination of Hobbs and Pocock, each taking three wickets, proved too much for the Pakistan side. They were all out for 263 and followed on 212 behind. We were looking for victory when they lost four wickets for 124 and Asif, their last recognized batsman, came in at number six. But that was almost as far as we got.

We did take four more wickets before the match ended that day, but only after Asif and Majid Khan had brushed us aside with a 167 run partnership in less than two and a half hours. They just carved us all around the Dacca Stadium to the delight of the local spectators, who lit fires on the concrete terracing to celebrate the saving of the game. Majid was cool and calculating, and Asif was the destroyer. He hit one six and thirteen fours in his 117 run innings, made in 150 minutes, before he was caught off the left-arm spin of Bissex who had earlier bowled Majid when the batsman was five short of a deserved century.

The study of the two teams on that tour is quite revealing. Nine of the MCC Under-25 party went on to play full Test cricket, and Brearley would probably have done so if he had not left the game during his middle twenties to continue his studies for another three years. And no less than eleven of the Pakistan players we met in the official representative matches also became full Test players. I thought Asif Iqbal led that side with imagination and aggression, and will make a good Pakistan Test captain before very long.

John Shepherd, too, has proved a wonderful capture. He is a very good cricketer in our conditions, and I am surprised he has not played for the West Indies more, especially after his record against England in 1969. In conditions where the ball encourages swing or the wicket is a little damp he can prove almost unplayable. One will never know how much he has been handicapped by the back injury he received during that 1969 series.

From the way he bowls these days I should think he must have to nurse his back a little, because he does not use it as much in his action. I've also noted that in the last season he has developed an extra twirl in his arm movement as though he is seeking that little extra pace.

He is one of the Kent players whose batting record has been upset by being constantly moved up and down the order. I should imagine that he would have scored many more runs if he had held a regular middle order position, instead of often finding himself lower down when the Test players have returned from international duty.

When he is in the mood Shep is a powerful striker of the ball, as Northants players will recall to their cost when they met up with him at Folkestone in 1968. That was the first season of bonus points, and we picked up eight in our first innings thanks to Shep's tremendous burst and two hefty contributions from Ealham and Dixon.

Shep was in for less than three hours, but that was long enough for him to make 170, a career best score, with five sixes and twenty-four other boundary strokes. There was just no way the Northants bowlers could pin him down or cut off his flow of runs, especially when he opened his shoulders to drive the ball over long on. Ealham doesn't believe in wasting time either, and he caught Shep's mood when the pair were in together. The result was a 164 run sixth wicket partnership in 95 minutes. It did not finish there, for Dixon then scored 82 not out at a run a minute before Colin Cowdrey called off the hunt with our score 458 for nine, made at four and a half runs an over. We picked up 21 points in winning that match by 75 runs.

Norman Graham is another whose work over the years has proved invaluable, a bowler who keeps going until he is ready to drop. He must also rank as one of the most nervous cricketers I have seen before a match starts. Before a big match the tension really gets to him, and yet it all vanishes when he steps on the field. He may take a bit of stick now and again – as most bowlers do – when he returns for his second spell in limited over games, but I should imagine he has been more economical than 95 per cent of opening bowlers in his first four or five over spell.

He doesn't do much with the ball and doesn't try to. He appreciates that his main weapon is the bounce he can extract with his great height, and that is often sufficient when combined with a good length and line. His golden year was in 1967 when he finished with 104 wickets, taking 22 of them in one week at

Tunbridge Wells. He took twelve for 77 in our 208 run defeat of Sussex and followed with ten for 64 when we beat Worcestershire by 202 runs in the next match.

One Kent player who has been an enormous source of encouragement and help to me has been Alan Knott. What a great comfort it has been for me to know that day in and day out I have been bowling with the best wicketkeeper in the world at the other end, ready to take advantage of any error I may cause the batsman to make. He has kept to me so regularly over the years that he knows what type of delivery I am going to bowl before even I have made up my mind.

We've grown up together in cricket from our schooldays, when we played with each other for the Kent Schools Cricket Association, and he has been a great help to me off the field. We've spent hours and hours together discussing my bowling and various batsmen, hours scheming and devising ways of getting them out. He is a wonderful judge of how a batsman is playing, how the wicket is reacting, and what type of bowler to put on. Ray Illingworth relied a great deal on Knotty's assessment of the situation from behind the stumps.

We have never devised any set signals between us, but he always gets the message across to me when he wants me to bowl a particular type of delivery. If he fancies the batsman will be in trouble against a slower delivery he raises his eyes to ask for one to be tossed up. If he thinks a fast yorker will do the trick he points down to the ground and so on.

Naturally I have seen him take all manner of catches, but his greatest standing up was Sardesai's wicket in England's final Test against India at the Oval in 1971. Sardesai had gone well forward against me in an attempt to kill the turn, but the ball just did enough to find the edge of the bat. It squeezed out quickly and was dropping fast, yet Knotty somehow dived well to his right to pick it up, just getting his hand between the ball and the ground.

How he managed to move so far is a marvel, because Sardesai was blocking his vision and he could not have seen the ball until after the deflection. It was a tribute to his speed of thought and agility.

The best I have seen him take standing back was Bill Lawry's wicket at Lord's in 1968 when Australia were dismissed for 78 in a drawn game. It was in the first innings, when Lawry played forward against David Brown and got an inside edge. Knotty was moving to his left to cover the expected line of the ball and then had to throw himself to his right down the leg side – Lawry being a left-hander – to scoop up the ball. He travelled many a yard to reach that one.

He did the same at Folkestone during 1974 to dismiss Kallicharran in the John Player League match against Warwickshire. At that stage we did not have a slip, and Kallicharran deliberately played the ball down towards third man. With no slip Kallicharran said afterwards he was not worried that the shot was a little uppish. He hadn't counted on Knotty, who took off and was still airborne when he clutched the ball in his outstretched left hand, five feet off the ground and in front of where third slip would have been standing. It was a wonderful effort.

Cricket with Kent has brought me so much pleasure outside the winning of the championship in 1970 and the victories in the various limited over competitions. Most players have sides they traditionally do well against, and Sussex and Yorkshire have been my sides.

Apart from my debut match in 1963 against Yorkshire, and my seven wicket performance in their second innings the following year, another match against them which I remember well was in 1966 at Harrogate. It was the final match of the season, and Yorkshire started it knowing that victory would give them the championship yet again. The weather was foul throughout, and at one time it became so dark that car headlights had to be used to help the ground staff mop up the surroundings. I took four for 105 as Boycott masterminded their first innings 210, and followed with seven for 30 when they were dismissed for 109 in their second innings, giving me eleven in the match. But they still managed to win by 24 runs. Nothing stopped Yorkshire in those days.

In 1971 it didn't seem to matter how I bowled against them, I would take a wicket. Kent beat Yorkshire twice that season by an innings. At Canterbury we won in two days. We made 250, and I took five for 19 in Yorkshire's first innings of 89 and five for 41 when they were bowled out a second time for 131. That same summer I took nine wickets in the match when our innings victory took three days at Bradford.

It was on that same ground the following season that I took eleven wickets in the match. My return was only three for 26 in the first innings but I managed eight for 70 in the second when we won by an innings and 30 runs inside two days.

This did not compare with my match haul of fourteen against Sussex in 1967 at Hastings, when I took seven wickets in each innings in our victory by an innings and 136 runs. In all, the wickets cost me 82 runs.

It was against Sussex that I took nine for 28 in 1964 and I came near to beating that in 1973 at Hastings. It was Tony Greig's first match as Sussex skipper and he had the misfortune of seeing his side bowled out twice for a total of 121 runs on a rain affected wicket. We had batted first and scored 282 for five before the rain got at the wicket. In the Sussex first innings of 67 I took five for 43, and in their second innings of 54 I emerged from my 10.1 overs with eight wickets for nine runs.

During the late 1960s, one or two of the occasional grounds used for cricketing weeks around the county received unfavourable wicket reports, which led to a couple being struck off the first class list for a while. This in turn led to suspicions that some wickets could have been prepared to suit me. Just as some critics have claimed that I am not such an effective bowler overseas, others have also said I am not the same danger force when bowling outside the Kent borders.

In my defence I should like to quote some figures worked out by Bill Frindall, the BBC radio cricket statistician who did a complete breakdown on my returns after my first seven years in first class cricket.

The breakdown revealed that of the 720 wickets I had taken for Kent in that period, I had won more than 52 per cent of them outside the county. I had played 91 matches in Kent resulting in 344 wickets, and taken 376 wickets outside Kent in 82 matches.

The figures did not end there. Frindall produced another breakdown of my figures in all matches, including those taken overseas on MCC tours. In Britain up until that time I had taken 815 wickets in 197 matches at an average cost of 17.41. Overseas I had played in 18 matches taking 68 wickets at an average cost of 17.01. The breakdown revealed that although my wickets overseas took an average seven deliveries longer to acquire, they did not cost as much per wicket as those taken in this country where the conditions suit me better. That will surprise many people. I must admit I was surprised myself.

12. WE ARE THE CHAMPIONS

From bottom to top in a few weeks . . . A Cheltenham victory . . . The batsmanship of Mike Denness . . . Surrey cliff-hanger . . . Run-feasts against Notts and Leics.

Being dropped by England is not an experience I have enjoyed, but it can have its compensations. It happened to me in 1970 after I had played in the first three international matches against the Rest of the World side. That was my lot for the summer as far as England was concerned.

My compensation came in being able to devote the rest of the six weeks of the season to helping Kent swing along towards the championship. We went through the remaining thirteen matches of the summer unbeaten after being bottom of the table on July 1st of that summer. It was a remarkable run which resulted in the championship returning to Kent in our centenary year and for the first time since 1913.

When Colin Cowdrey's duties with the England team finished in mid-August and he was available to lead us for the last four matches, three of them at home, the scene was set for a grand finale.

At that stage the championship was in sight, but still pretty far away. The next three matches brought us within touching distance when we picked up 60 points, needing only a handful from our final match of the season against Surrey at the Oval to prevent Lancashire pipping us at the post.

Possibly the turning point had been reached before Colin came back for those last four matches. It might have been the match against Gloucestershire at Cheltenham which convinced us all we were championship material, when we had to score 320 runs to win in our fourth innings – an almost unheard-of feat on Cheltenham's wicket, which had proved a haven for spinners in general for some seasons, and for Gloucestershire's off-spinning duo of Allen and Mortimore in particular.

Perhaps the turning point was reached even earlier: at a team meeting at Maidstone when we attempted to find the cause of our dismal start to that summer, and the reason why we were lagging behind most other county sides who, on paper, lacked the collective ability of Kent.

One of the major reasons, we decided, was the bonus point system which had been introduced two seasons earlier. We were just not approaching the matter in the right way. The outcome of that team meeting at Maidstone was to launch an all-out assault on batting bonus points and Mike Denness, who led the side when Colin was away on England duty, saw to it that they were earned. In doing so he set a wonderful example himself in his own batting, and it was just the encouragement Asif Iqbal needed to produce his quickfire methods, with the odd power burst from Alan Ealham. Again, these three worked wonders for Kent's fielding that summer.

It was Denness and Ealham who paved the way for Kent's second win of the season in the first week of July, which was the launching point for our second half recovery. They were supported by the bowlers in gaining that victory over Essex at Harlow. I missed that one, being away playing for England together with Luckhurst, Cowdrey and Knott.

That match was a remarkable reversal of fortunes because Essex, in the top half of the table, had beaten us by five wickets only a week earlier. They had no chance in the return, with Denness scoring an undefeated 167 and Ealham making 88, sharing a 164 run partnership in two and a half hours after four wickets had gone down for 65. Our batting bonus points were limited to three, but our total of 330 for seven declared was sufficient for victory. Essex just failed to save the follow on, with Shepherd taking five for 41, and started their second innings 151 behind. They were all out for 127 this time, and 40 of those runs came in an unlikely last wicket partnership between East and Acfield after Graham had destroyed the early batting with six for 67.

The victory lifted Kent off the bottom of the table, but the important message had come from the batting of Denness and Ealham who had shown what could be achieved with an aggressive

It took me nine years to get the wicket of Gary Sobers for the first time but he had no trouble picking up mine now and again, clean bowling me at Headingley in 1969.

Back goes the off stump and out goes Gary Sobers. It was only the second time in my career I had captured Sobers' wicket, and it helped speed England's victory in Trinidad in April, 1974, to square the series.

Captain Ray Illingworth swings round to watch me grab a return catch from Charlie Davis at Headingley in 1969, the most controversial Test catch of my career which starts a West Indies collapse and helps England to victory.

I've been fortunate to have the best wicketkeeper in the world, Alan Knott, taking my bowling for both club and country. His catching is superb as he shows here diving to his right to dismiss Viswanath in the Test against India at Lord's in 1974.

David Lloyd swoops to catch Wasim Raja at Lord's in 1974 and I'm off on my eight wicket trail during the Pakistan second innings.

Receiving a decanter and glasses from the Duke of Kent to mark Kent winning the County Championship in 1970.

Captain Mike Denness and one of our all-round heroes Asif, both shouldered high by delighted colleagues after we had won the Benson and Hedges Cup in 1973 at Lord's after beating Worcestershire.

approach even on a wicket which was helping the bowlers throughout.

When Kent went into that match we had only 20 batting bonus points to our credit from nine matches. Only four other county sides had scored less. By the end of the summer only one other side – Lancashire – could match our total batting points of 77. Not only did the aggressive batting policy we pursued during the remainder of the summer boost our batting bonus points but it gave us far more time in which to bowl out the opposition to bring the extra 10 points for victory.

I was prevented by injury from rejoining the Kent side immediately after I had been dropped from the England team, Sobers having split one of my fingers in the Rest of the World match at Trent Bridge. So I was out of the John Player League match against Sussex at Hove, the only game I've missed apart from Test calls. Not that Kent needed me over those three days on a wicket which helped the faster bowler. Although Sussex had Snow, the combination of Shepherd, Brown and Dye proved more effective in taking Kent to a ten wicket victory.

The first victory I had anything to do with in Kent's home run that year was against Somerset at Weston. I took five wickets in Somerset's second innings by – critics please note – deliberately tossing the ball up in the air.

Bob Woolmer had taken six for 53 in helping to dismiss Somerset for 211 in their first innings and a century by Denness had helped us gain a 52 run first innings lead on a wicket which was now taking spin. It meant a long uphill climb by Somerset to get out of trouble and we were frightened that they would not leave us sufficient time to knock off the runs we would require in the second innings.

Somerset had started well in their second innings with Virgin – now with Northants – and Clarkson passing 50 before Colin suggested that I should throw the ball up and give it some air. It helped to bring about an astonishing collapse, with the last nine wickets falling for 43 runs in 75 minutes, five to me and four to Graham Johnson's off-spin.

We won by ten wickets with plenty of time to spare in the end, and I must admit I enjoyed the experience of flighting the ball. Despite those five wickets for 40 runs, though, I never felt completely easy doing it. It might be all right for Somerset batsmen on a wicket taking spin, I thought, but it wouldn't do for Sobers and the like on a plum Test wicket.

From there we travelled to Cheltenham and the most outstanding victory of that summer in my opinion and, I should think, in the opinion of everybody there. Not only had we lost Cowdrey, Luckhurst and Knott to England, but we were also without Shepherd for that match, and he proved our leading wicket taker during the championship with 84 wickets for Kent, six more than I managed.

Gloucestershire batted first – as any side would do after winning the toss at Cheltenham – and scored 289, thanks mainly to a maiden championship century by Bissex, popularly known as 'Biscuit', and one of my pals of the MCC Under-25 tour to Pakistan four years earlier. He batted extremely well after Gloucestershire had lost their first three wickets for 33 runs. The wicket was taking some spin even then, and I managed to pick up six Gloucestershire wickets for 68 runs.

Before that day was over we had made a very unlucky start to our innings by losing Denness. He was out for a duck second ball, when he pulled a delivery against Smith's medium pace. The ball caught short leg Sullivan on the head, and ballooned up for Shepherd to take an easy catch at mid-wicket. Out went Denness. Out went Sullivan as well, taken off to hospital for treatment. Happily he had recovered later in the evening.

The Denness wicket was a severe blow. We had to make 140 to avoid being asked to follow on and were still 10 runs short when a mix up between Norman Graham and myself ended with Norman being run out. We were then 130 for nine with John Dye left, and we managed to hold out while we negotiated the necessary 10 runs. We had made exactly 140 when Mortimore had Dye caught to give him his fifth wicket in our innings.

Judging from the way we had batted in our first innings, Gloucestershire must have thought they were on to a good thing when they made 190 in their second innings – I took five for 82 this time – which left us needing 340 runs to win with a day and a bit to spare. That bit proved expensive too, for in the last over of the second day Woolmer, opening in place of the absent Luckhurst, fell to Allen's off spin with our score at 20.

So the target on the last day was 320 to win with nine wickets left, and it provided the setting for one of the finest innings I have seen from Denness and another from Asif. Mike was superb in helping Nicholls add 60 for the second wicket, but the turning point was the 105 Denness and Asif shared for the fifth wicket in 95 minutes, Denness selecting his scoring shots with great care while Asif chanced his arm. It ended when Denness, on 97, attempted to pull Mortimore to the mid-wicket boundary to reach his century but skied a catch. He deserved his three figures that day.

Asif reached his century mark before giving a catch behind against Allen, but despite the great efforts of these two we were still not clear. Victory was certainly in sight when we reached 329 with five wickets left. Only 11 runs were wanted now, but we lost four wickets making nine of them, and this time Dye had to hold on while Leary clinched the victory and 13 points. A remarkable match indeed. On the second day we had saved the follow on by one run with our last pair at the wicket, and won it the next day by scoring 340 runs the second time around. Victory by the slender margin of one wicket.

Mike Denness's innings that day reminded me of the two nineties he had scored the previous season against Somerset on a similar wicket at Bath. In each case, I think, the state of the wicket was the key to his success.

For many seasons he produced a number of innings which had an England look about them, but the lack of centuries over his career probably caused him to miss out at selection meetings when his record was compared with those of his main rivals, Luckhurst, Boycott, Edrich, Sharpe and Milburn. It must have given him a great boost to have scored those two Test centuries in successive innings against India in 1974, having gone fourteen Tests without reaching the magical three figures.

Mike has played some of his best innings against spinners on wickets helping the bowler. Those innings against Somerset, and the one against Gloucestershire in 1970, are typical examples. Another outstanding one, probably his best Test performance, was his 76 in the second innings at Madras during the 1972–73 tour to India.

But back to Kent on the championship trail. The next match after Cheltenham was a disappointment, when rain reduced the game against Northamptonshire to a draw. The following match, against Surrey at Blackheath, was another heart-stopping occasion.

We won it with just an over to spare, while Surrey only just failed in a sterling victory bid. This was a match in which Cowdrey expertly juggled with the bowling to keep Surrey fully committed to going for the runs even when their last pair were together. It was also a personal triumph for Johnson, who took six wickets in each Surrey innings with his off-spinners.

A century opening partnership by Luckhurst and Denness, followed by another century from Asif, enabled us to reach 325 – seven batting points – before Colin declared with three wickets down. By the end of the Surrey first innings we had a lead of 114, Johnson having taken his six wickets for 35. We batted until just after lunch on the third day before Colin declared again with the score 148 for four, setting Surrey the target of 263 to win in 203 minutes.

When the last hour started, the odds were slightly in our favour. Surrey needed another 61 runs while we had to capture four more wickets. Intikhab and Long were the not out batsmen, and both were looking quite secure.

The odds had swung even more in our favour by the time their last batsman, Pocock, walked to the wicket, Surrey then being 224 for nine with another 39 runs required. The danger man was Long at the other end, and it was a question of whether Pocock could give him the support he needed.

There were just two minutes to go on the clock when the end came, off the final ball of the twenty-first over we had bowled since the last hour started. And what an end! Pocock stepped down the wicket against Johnson and hit him powerfully into the vacant space at wide long off. It looked a six all the way. Then Asif struck. He had been stationed almost straight behind the bowler's arm, in the area where Surrey had already hit two sixes, but the moment the ball left Pocock's bat Asif was off. He sprinted at least twenty-five yards round the boundary just inside the ropes before sticking out his left hand to clutch the ball shoulder high.

It would have been a remarkable one-handed catch if the fielder had been stationed at that very spot, but to run twenty-five to thirty yards to achieve it was incredible. Only a fielder of Asif's outstanding sprinting ability could have done it. Some Surrey supporters criticized Pocock for making the blow, but he was absolutely right in his intentions. If it hadn't been for Asif,

Pocock would have scored a six which would have left Surrey requiring seven runs off the final over with Long having the strike. They would have been favourites to have done that.

A glance at the Surrey score card during their second innings is revealing. It shows just what I meant earlier in the book when I wrote that Cowdrey was a superb tactician when it came to feeding the opposition enough runs to keep them interested in a chase. Of the first eight Surrey batsmen, only one failed to reach double figures. All the other seven scored at least 20, but Long was the only player to pass 40. In other words, Cowdrey encouraged each one to play shots but snapped up their wickets the moment they showed signs of settling down to play the long innings Surrey needed from one player to secure the victory.

The Surrey game produced our fifth victory in ten matches, three of them worth twenty points or more. But there was no hope of getting twenty points once Sobers had started to wade into us in the next match against Nottinghamshire at Folkestone. Our only chance of keeping up with the championship contenders was by obtaining an outright victory. This we did in another nerve-tingling finish with eight balls to go.

Such an outcome seemed unlikely when Nottinghamshire, batting first, followed up a more than useful start with a torrent of runs from Sobers and Smedley. Smedley, an extremely correct and elegant player, although not very aggressive, made 92, but Sobers dashed to his century in just over two and a half hours, and hit two more sixes before he declared at the fall of Smedley's wicket. These two had added 203 runs for the fourth wicket, taking Nottinghamshire to 376 for four, while our reward had been one bowling bonus point plus considerable leather chasing. In addition we lost Denness before the day was through, and I found myself batting as night watchman. I did not last long the following morning, and with Halfyard bowling well we were 27 for five at one stage before Luckhurst found somebody to partner him. Ealham, Shepherd and Woolmer all had their spells in giving Luckhurst some comfort, while he made 156 before Cowdrey declared on 310 for seven, some 66 runs behind.

Sobers again batted well in Nottinghamshire's second innings, as did Bolus, which enabled Nottinghamshire to declare a second time in the match at 215 for six. So we had been set 282 to win in three hours. It was a stiff task, even though the wicket was good, but we had nothing to lose at that stage and Denness and Luckhurst accepted the challenge on our behalf by putting on 103 for the first wicket. Luckhurst was the first to go, and his place was taken by Asif as Cowdrey switched the batting order. The move worked. In the next fifty minutes Asif and Denness added 94 runs and were still together when the last hour was signalled with us still 112 runs from home.

The scoring now became even more frantic. Wickets started to fall too, but we managed to keep up with the clock. There were only two overs left when Knott went to the wicket, but he produced a burst of three scoring strokes which all went for four against Sobers. This took us to a three wicket victory with eight balls to spare.

Naturally we were in good heart for our following match, the last of the Folkestone week, against Leicestershire. We were entering the home straight now and nothing was going to stop Colin.

Thanks to a fine spell of bowling by Shepherd, who took five for 64, we gained our full allowance of five bonus bowling points when dismissing Leicestershire for 152. Then it was full steam ahead to get as many batting bonus points as possible.

Again we were away to a good start when Denness and Luckhurst opened with a 98 run stand, followed up by Johnson scoring 108 and Asif weighing in with a breezy 63. But my memory of that innings is of Shepherd going in near the end, and finding himself facing the medium fast bowling of Stringer, who came up to bowl the 85th over with us needing another 18 runs for our eighth batting point. Ten of the runs came off the first two balls as Shepherd smashed Stringer for a four and six, the first through and the second over long on. Then came a mid-over lull before Shepherd smashed another six and took two off the last ball to earn that extra point.

Colin finally declared with our score at 421, leaving Leicestershire wanting 269 to avoid an innings defeat. Before the close on that second day they lost three wickets making 97. The only resistance on the final morning was provided by Davison, who hit two sixes and nine fours in his 63. We won by an innings and 40 runs with time in hand. More important were the 23 points we picked up.

Those points took us to the top of the table, nine clear of the defending champions, Glamorgan, who had finished their programme. We had one more match to play. The only side with any chance of catching us was Lancashire in third place. They were eighteen points behind, which meant that six bonus points – seven at the outside – were needed from our final match against Surrey at the Oval to be absolutely sure. Lancashire's final match was also against Surrey at the Oval, immediately after our game.

In theory Surrey also had a chance. If they could restrict us to a handful of bonus points, do the same against Lancashire, and pick up 40 points from their last two matches they could still take the championship. But it was asking a lot.

The weather delayed the start of that final match until the afternoon of the first day and, not surprisingly in the conditions, Cowdrey put Surrey in on winning the toss. With bonus points the main consideration, he thought five would be easier to take through bowling rather than batting.

In fact we managed only four for bowling. A fifth would have been a certainty when the Surrey ninth wicket fell at 151, but Stewart then declared. That left us needing another four to be on the safe side and, appropriately, they were earned on the second day by Cowdrey himself when he scored his third championship century of the summer. There was still a day of our season to go, but it really ended that night with the county championship ours, in addition to the one gained by the second eleven side, and our second placing in the John Player League. The Gillette Cup had been our one disappointment that summer. We had reached the third round only to lose to our old rivals, Sussex.

We all felt that the championship was just the start. Of the side which had played in the final match at the Oval only Cowdrey and Luckhurst were over thirty which meant that Kent possessed a group of players who were going to be around together for several years to come. We were looking forward to bigger and better things. And they duly arrived.

13. ONE-DAY CRICKET, THE GOOD AND THE NOT SO GOOD

Unfair to spinners! . . . The Gillette Cup final of 1974 . . . Lancashire rivals . . . Key semi-finals . . . Three amazing one-day games.

Most people would have expected me to be delighted when the growing influence of limited over cricket brought the John Player League into operation in 1969. If ever a competition seemed designed to suit my style of bowling down to the ground, this was it.

The best way to win is, of course, by bowling the opposition out cheaply. The second best is to keep the opposing batsmen so bogged down that their average striking rate is less than three an over. This I have sometimes been able to do.

Yet I was very suspicious when the John Player League started. I had a number of reservations, partly brought about by Kent's comparative lack of success in the Gillette Cup over the longer course of 60 overs. Admittedly we won the Gillette Cup in 1967 when beating Somerset in the final at Lord's. But that was also the first year we had managed to overcome another championship side in the competition.

My chief worry concerning limited over cricket was that in order to save runs I had to give runs away. That may sound a little Irish but it does sum up the situation. And I hate being forced to give even one run away.

In the Gillette Cup competition in particular, orthodox fields are set at the start. There may not be quite the number of close to the wicket fielders that you would find at the start of a first class match, but the majority of the fielders are in a position to save one run. As soon as a batsman has a dip and hits one over the top, the ring is pushed back to save the fours. With every pace the fielder takes backwards, the easier it is for the batsmen to take singles in their own good time.

From the team point of view it is the only policy. Far better to give two, three, or even four singles away in an over than leave the batsmen with a chance of swinging merrily for a couple of fours. But I must say I dislike bowling to well-spread fielders. Whatever the match, I like to feel I am attacking.

The other worrying aspect of the introduction of the John Player League was the fate of spin bowlers in general. The first six seasons of the Gillette Cup had shown that the great majority of county sides dropped their recognized spinners and brought in extra seamers for the one day game. Only the very best of the spinners survived.

Would the trend continue and limit the influence of spinners on the game as a whole? It has of course. It is a tragedy that even today such genuine slow bowlers as Ray East (Essex), Bishen Bedi (Northants) and Jack Birkenshaw (Leicestershire) often find themselves sitting it out on a Sunday. The spinners who do play regularly cannot really be called spinners on a Sunday.

Pocock, for instance, is a fine bowler and one of the biggest spinners of the ball in the game – that's why he suffers from a split spinning finger – but on Sunday he virtually bowls seam up with swinging yorkers into the block hole, frequently from round the wicket. Intikhab was forced to abandon his leg spin in 1974 in the one day internationals against England and resort to seamers, while Lancashire's Simmons has not earned his nick-name 'Flat Jack' for nothing.

Despite the obvious weaknesses in this form of cricket, I have come to enjoy it much more now. Our success has obviously helped, but so has the backing which this type of cricket has gained from supporters, and which produces such a healthy atmosphere that the players can't help but be lifted. But strangely enough, I am finding it more difficult to bowl in limited over cricket now, although I am obviously much more experienced in the art required.

So are the batsmen. My line has always been to push the ball in the direction of the leg stump against the right-handed bats-men, tucking them up and forcing them to play on the leg side. But today more and more batsmen are standing outside their leg stump and are still able to hit through the offside. This is where

Luckhurst has become such an expert. Bowlers have found it almost impossible to pin him down.

He has been the key figure in our success over the last three or four seasons. So has Asif. Another vital factor has been the very high quality of our fielding, not only in terms of catching and ground work but in returning the ball over the top of the stumps. The Gillette Cup final against Lancashire in 1974 was a splendid example of fielding at its best.

Although I was pacing the dressing room nervously in the last half hour of that match, I never really felt we would lose. Not even when we lost three wickets for the addition of one run. Now we were 53 for four in reply to their 118 on a wicket which produced unpredictable bounce and was always doing enough to leave the medium-paced seamer in control.

Not even when we were 89 for six, and still needing another 30 runs to win with only James Graham-Brown, myself, and Norman Graham to come. I always had the feeling we were in charge.

The build-up to that match was rather strange, with the bookmakers making Kent the favourites but most of the cricket writers tipping Lancashire, largely because of the past results between the two county sides and the fact that we were missing Asif and Julien, two of our key figures. We had met Lancashire in various stages of the competition but never managed to beat them before. I think people lost sight of the fact that we had looked likely winners against Lancashire in the 1971 final and would surely have beaten them in the 1972 semi-final at Old Trafford but for the weather.

We lost that 1971 final because of one catch which dismissed Asif when he looked certain to complete the century which would have taken us to victory. With Clive Lloyd scoring 66, and Simmons and Hughes sharing an unbeaten 45 run partnership for the eighth wicket, Lancashire reached 224 for seven off their 60 overs, a highly respectable score.

It looked good enough when we lost four wickets making 68, before Asif and Knott settled down and put us back on equal terms. Then a mix-up resulted in Knotty being run out with the score 105. That was when Asif took charge, revelling in the atmosphere and showing, like Basil d'Oliveira, that he is a big occasion player. I can never imagine Asif making runs before a deserted house at Dartford. Put him before 25,000 spectators and he is in his element.

He was 11 short of his century when he put the ball in the air – one of the few occasions during his innings – as he aimed to drive Simmons to the deserted space of long off. It seemed safe enough, a certain four, until Bond jumped, stretched out his hand, and pulled off a tumbling catch.

It was a catch which changed the whole match. At the moment Asif struck the ball Lancashire were feeling a little down. They, too, thought Asif's century was inevitable. But when the ball nestled in Bond's hands they were back on top of the world and we slumped. We might still have won it, but we lost our last three wickets for three runs and were all out for 200.

When we met Lancashire in the semi-final the following summer they also made 224, batting first with little Harry Pilling scoring 70. Nothing will shake my belief that we would have won that match but for the weather.

Overnight rain put back the start until after lunch, and it was 5.30 before we were able to begin our reply with the clouds thickening up again and the light fading rapidly. We lost Luckhurst and Johnson in making 34, but then Denness and Cowdrey teamed up brilliantly despite the gloom. Three times the umpires told the two of them they thought the conditions were unfair, and suggested that play should be abandoned for the day, but having got into a rhythm they naturally wanted to stay on and make the most of it. Only when Cowdrey was leg before against Lee, with the score 110 for three, did Denness reluctantly agree to end play for the day.

The interruption to our innings meant that we had to start cold on the second day. We had lost the momentum we had been gathering the night before and the Lancashire bowlers were also fresh. To keep up with the required run rate that second morning some indiscreet shots were played – mainly sweeping at Simmons – and we finally lost by seven runs when I was stumped in the sixtieth over.

Up to the end of 1974 we have played in four finals at Lords – three times in the Gillette Cup and once in the Benson and Hedges – but the match which worried me most on the final trail was the Gillette semi-final against Somerset at Canterbury in 1974. In the end we won by three wickets with more than two overs to spare. I've played in many tight matches but rarely a tighter one than this, although our margin of victory was quite a healthy one in the end.

We had limited Somerset to 154 – Close running himself out to add to their problems – but the early loss of Luckhurst, who was out when he had scored 8, worried me. When we sank to 91 for five I must confess I thought it was all over. Not even a 29 run partnership between Knott and Ealham, and another worth 14 between Ealham and Woolmer, reduced my worries. But finally Woolmer and Elms steered us to victory, scoring the last 21 runs together.

I think the tension got to me that day – a tension which was missing at Lord's in the final, with the match delayed until the Monday and the ground only just over half full. Canterbury was packed for that semi-final, and such was the atmosphere, tension and pressure that two spectators died from heart attacks during the afternoon.

In 1973 I never had any doubts about the outcome of the Benson and Hedges final against Worcestershire, once Luckhurst got going after a very sticky start. At first tight bowling restricted us to 34 for two off our first twenty overs. But then Luckhurst got to work. Just as one catch had ruined the 1971 Gillette Cup final for us, so one shot changed the Benson and Hedges final in 1973. Boldly Luckhurst placed his left leg down the track against d'Oliveira and struck him for a mighty six over long on. That broke the ice. Worcestershire's grip on the game melted from that moment as Luckhurst and Asif mixed sensible hitting with superb running between the wickets to add 116 runs in 28 overs. We finally made 225 for seven off the 55 overs.

The only time Worcestershire at all bothered us was when Gifford and d'Oliveira put on 79, but they were still facing a stiff run rate even at the end of this stand with only four wickets left. In an attempt to upset our bowling, they decided to keep a left-hand/right-hand partnership at the wicket most of the time by juggling with their batting order. It was good thinking. It meant that we constantly had to adjust our bowling line, sometimes two or three times an over, which no bowler likes doing. It also meant that two of their main limited over scorers, d'Oliveira and Yardley, had to bat at seven and eight respectively. When d'Oliveira entered, for instance, Worcestershire were 98 for five and their target had grown to 128 off their remaining twenty overs.

D'Oliveira, naturally, rose to the challenge with an innings of 47, and I was a very relieved player when I took the catch which finally ended his stay when Worcestershire's score had grown to 168. There was nothing difficult about the catch. That was why I was so relieved when it stuck. I would have had no excuse for missing it.

The ball before, d'Oliveira had swung Asif over the mid-wicket region for a six, and now he was attempting a repeat stroke. He failed to get hold of it properly in his eagerness and skied it up to widish mid-on where I just had to take a couple of steps forward. His departure saw the end of Worcestershire's challenge.

The one time Worcestershire did frighten me a little was the final John Player League match against them at Canterbury in September, 1972. We had to win that match to pip Leicestershire and capture the title for the first time. Leicestershire had completed their programme the Sunday before, and were sitting on top of the table with 44 points. We started our final game against Worcestershire three points behind.

My worry was whether we would be able to control the flow of runs when Ron Headley and Alan Ormrod joined together to score 73 off 17 overs for the third wicket. Unfortunately most of those runs came against me. Worcestershire totalled 190 for five off their 40 overs, and I emerged with my worst ever Sunday return of one for 61 off my eight overs. But Luckhurst with 67, and Nicholls scoring 46, covered my embarrassment by pacing our five wicket victory with two overs to spare. The title was ours, and we ran away with it the following summer. The whole thing was sown up before the end of July for us to win it again and in record time.

There are three one-day games for Kent which stick out in my mind over the years – three of the most astonishing games in which I have played. Two of them took place in 1967 on our way to the final win against Somerset.

The first was against Surrey at the Oval in the third round, after we had beaten Essex in the second. I remember it distinctly for one good reason. I didn't bat or bowl! Poor Surrey didn't stand a chance that day once Colin Cowdrey had given Alan Dixon the ball. He finished with seven wickets for 15 runs.

He was brought into the attack after Edwards and Edrich had given Surrey a 31 run start, and took a wicket in each of his first five overs. When he had finished his twelve over stint only two wickets remained, and Sayer came back to finish Surrey off for 74. I wasn't needed that day at all, for we scored the runs for the loss of four wickets to claim our semi-final place against Sussex.

Obviously Alan Dixon won the man of the match award during the Surrey game. There was nobody else who stood a chance. Against Sussex the award went to Colin Cowdrey. But Kent's hero that day, in my book, was undoubtedly John Shepherd with Colin a close second.

Shep was batting number three and found himself at the wicket with Kent having only three runs on the board. Snow was really letting himself go, and quickly accounted for Denness. In fact the Sussex attack of Snow and Tony Buss was looking very menacing, but Shepherd launched into it from the moment he arrived at the crease, and turned the match our way by scoring 77 out of a 133 run partnership with Luckhurst for the second wicket before he was leg-before against Bates.

There is no doubt that Colin's innings of 78 – the same score as Luckhurst – was a gem. He took only ten overs to reach 50, and batted only eighteen overs during which he shared a 57 run blitz in six overs with Knotty. His timing and placing was immaculate, and he had the Canterbury crowd purring as our score rose to 293 for five off our 60 overs. But the fact remains that the stage had been set for him by Shepherd. Scoring 78 when your side has 138 runs on the board is far easier than making 77 when there are only three runs on the board and the opposition is on top.

Sussex stood no chance, despite some bold hitting by Parks and Greig, and were all out for 175, their last three wickets falling at the same score. That was a memorable victory for us because it is the only time Kent have beaten Sussex in the Gillette. They even surprised us in 1973 when they knocked us out of the Gillette after we had already won the Benson and Hedges Cup and had the John Player title in the bag. We thought the one-day treble was on for us that season.

The other match I remember well was the John Player League match against Middlesex at Folkestone in 1972 – the year we first won the Sunday title. It serves as a reminder that in cricket no match is ever won or lost until the final delivery has been sent down.

There was just no way we could lose that match and not gain our fifth win of the summer in six matches to take over the League leadership. Or so it seemed. After losing half their side for 40 Middlesex had recovered to 127 all out in the fortieth over, Murray and Jones sharing in a seventh wicket partnership of 54. Victory appeared a pure formality when Nicholls and Johnson opened with a 51 run partnership, and again when Ealham and Nicholls took the score to 109 for four before they were parted.

By the time the 37th over started we were 126 for six, with two runs needed to win, four wickets left, and 24 balls to go. Four points were in the bag. We thought so, Middlesex thought so. The crowd thought so. But we lost by one run. We were all out for 126.

The panic started with a mix-up between Nicholls and Julien which saw Nicholls run out for 54. That was 126 for seven. I went to the wicket next to join Julien, who was then caught behind by Murray off the bowling of Selvey. That was 126 for eight. Still two runs wanted with two more overs to go.

That brought Asif in to join me. He was batting low because he had been taken ill with a bout of malaria, and was only going to appear in an emergency. The emergency had arisen, but Asif was too ill to cope and Selvey bowled him for nought. That was 126 for nine, and last man Norman Graham was threading his way through the astonished crowd to join me at the wicket.

He survived the rest of that over. I received the first two balls of the final over from Black as I waited for a delivery I could push for the two runs, but was leg-before to the third ball. We were 126 all out. It was all over, with four wickets having gone down without addition.

It is happenings such as these which make cricket such a fascinating game. And why I am thankful to be a part of it. But there is so much more. I hope I have many more years left in the game. I'm still young enough to look forward to possibly another ten years at county level.

If anybody has a leaning towards cricket but is unsure of taking the next step, I have one recommendation. Give it a go. I did, with the full backing and encouragement of my family, but it is always wise to have another career in mind as a stand-by.

My parents backed me, but they also warned that if I had not made the grade by the time I was twenty-one then I should look for another career while I was still young enough. That is sound advice.

It is not only the playing of cricket which makes it such a wonderful sport, but also the friendships and comradeship which result. Not just among your colleagues and rivals but also with people outside the game and in various parts of the world. I'd like to thank all of them for helping to make the last twelve years of my life as rich as they have been.

14. MCC IN AUSTRALASIA, 1974/5

Lillee and Thomson, two great fast bowlers . . .
'Bouncers' and short-pitched deliveries . . .
MCC lose the Ashes . . . The Future.

It sounds idiotic to say that there were a couple of times in Australia last winter when, with a bat in my hand, I held an unfair advantage playing the fast bowling of Jeff Thomson and Dennis Lillee, because of action taken by the umpires, telling Lillee and Thomson to pitch the ball further up to me.

That probably sums up the whole complex situation over the one great issue to emerge from the loss of the Ashes on the tour – the question of short-pitched and intimidatory bowling and how the umpires should deal with it.

There is no doubt that on many occasions during the six match Test series our batsmen – tail-enders included – were more concerned with the matter of self preservation than scoring runs or even just staying at the wicket. But that is nothing new in the game of cricket.

It has happened before whenever a country throws up two fast bowlers at the same time who complement each other. When they do, that country is on a winner.

Make no mistake, Lillee and Thomson are a fearsome combination as you will see again. I'm quite prepared – having had to face them – to accept that they are the most destructive pair working together since the war, though I never saw Lindwall and Miller. I am sure Thomson spurred Lillee on to greater things, Lillee fighting to establish himself again after his injury, and Thomson, the new boy, raw to Test cricket, fighting to gain recognition. On pure technical ability, Lillee is a far better bowler, possessing more control and an ability in his classic action to swing the ball, though possibly not as consistently quick as his partner. Yet as the tour went on Lillee was bowling as fast as ever, having proved to himself that his back could stand up to the strain.

Thomson shook us all by his pace and his strength. It was remarkable the way he was able to come back in the late afternoon and still bowl as quick as ever but I felt at times he wasn't quite as confident when operating with a new ball. He would still come in strongly at you at 5 o'clock in the afternoon and it left us wondering where he got his stamina from. He was the more dangerous to face too. Whereas Lillee's line was consistently off stump and just outside, Thomson, possibly through lack of experience and because of his action, at times appeared to lose a certain amount of control and it proved very difficult to pick up the line of the ball when facing him.

They did bowl short for much of the series particularly against our recognised batsmen. They also dug it in against the rest of us from time to time. It couldn't have been a pretty sight for any England supporter watching us trying to get out of the way. It wasn't particularly pleasant out in the middle either.

It brought howls of protest from some people, bitter condemnation from others and demands that something should be done before somebody is killed in the Test arena. That, of course, almost happened in New Zealand when their last batsman Ewan Chatfield needed the kiss of life to revive him on the field after he had edged a short-pitched delivery from Peter Lever on to his head – the only short-pitched delivery Lever had bowled at him. I could not help but think how ironic it was that this should happen at that stage of our tour when we'd all been ducking and weaving for four months in Australia.

What happened to Chatfield highlights the whole problem when people demand that bouncers should be limited. Can more action be taken to provide safeguards for the batsmen or tail-enders? Obviously the fewer bouncers bowled during the day, the less chance of a batsman being injured. But if only one bouncer is bowled – as in Chatfield's case – it could turn out to be the fatal one.

In that last paragraph I changed the terminology deliberately. I used the description 'bouncer' instead of 'short-pitched delivery' and this is where the confusion arises when demands for action are made. And where the law makers will run into trouble when any attempt is made to sort out the problem by legislation.

The true bouncer is the dangerous weapon. The ball that rears up and comes through head high. The one that could bring about a fatality if it strikes home. Nobody likes seeing a batsman hurt, especially when he's been hit on the head. Can you cut out the bouncer? Can you limit the number of bouncers in an over? What finer sight is there in cricket than when a batsman hooks a bouncer? Quite often the difference between a rib tickling short-of-a-length delivery and a head high bouncer is only a matter of a few inches or so when it comes to where the ball has actually pitched. In England it can pitch in almost an identical place but because of the uneven bounce of our wickets, life as a batsman can be quite treacherous against the real quick bowler bowling just short of a length.

It was the short-pitched delivery, not the bouncer, which actually caused the discomfort in Australia, the fractured ribs of John Edrich when he was hit by Lillee during the fourth Test in Sydney. The ball which resulted in many of us suffering from chest pains, broken fingers, and battered knuckles. Can you ban a ball short of a length which rears up around rib high? Can this be deemed an unfair weapon? I don't think so. Perhaps at times we played a little low and didn't allow for the extra bounce of Australian wickets.

Or can you even make legislation to ban their use against tail-end batsmen? Again I believe the answer is no. I don't like facing them. Nobody does. But I expect them if I have been hanging around the crease for half an hour or so, standing in the way of the opposition and victory. I've got no complaints on that score. Even when facing Lillee or Thomson.

I know some English critics complained that the umpires might have taken a firmer stand against the Australian bowlers. At least twice, however, they warned Lillee and Thomson for bowling bouncers at me. In a way they were a little harsh. In each case it was the first one I had received in that particular over. Perhaps I looked as if I couldn't defend myself, but cricket at Test level is a hard business. It was from that point that I knew I could look to play forward a little more against them for a few deliveries before they would dare slip in another one. That is giving me an advantage over the bowler. No batsman should be able to make up his mind what stroke he is going to play before a ball is bowled. I'd hate to think a batsman could do that against me.

I think we found ourselves in Australia wishing that we'd been lucky enough to have Lillee and Thomson on our side. After all, there was some short-pitched bowling from us too, and four years previously we had John Snow to dish out the medicine, when we won the series in Australia 2-nil. The Australian never forgets, as he has shown us. Perhaps next time we'll have a couple of quick bowlers to do battle with them, as good and as effective as Lillee and Thomson. Let's hope we can show them that the Englishman also never forgets. One thing for sure it will always be the quick bowlers who will win you a series in Australia.

I've deliberately spent a little time examining the subject of short-pitched bowling because it was one of the most talked about features of the series. And it is one for which there is no ready made solution, except to rely on the discretion and common sense of the umpires.

There is one thing that will be done, possibly, before very long. The day is not very far away when batsmen will wear protective head gear, rather like jockeys or even of the baseball type. I know one or two of our batsmen are now investigating various types of protective headgear to find out whether they are comfortable, too heavy, or obstruct vision in any way. A cricket outfitter who comes up with a suitable one will be on to a good thing.

There is also likely to be an extension of protective clothing worn in addition to pads, gloves and box. For a long time Colin Cowdrey has worn a type of chest protector on occasions – ever since he took a battering from Wes Hall and Charlie Griffith. In Australia one or two of the boys also had one made for them by the team's physiotherapist Bernard Thomas to protect the ribs and chest.

Whatever might have been said or written about the bowling of Lillee and Thomson last winter there is one thing nobody on the England side will deny. They were just too good for us. Too good because they were too fast and were still able to swing and move the ball around off the wicket. We just haven't got the experience and technique at present against that speed to cope on their wickets with that little extra bounce.

I would like to see if Lillee and Thomson could maintain their pace over a five year period of English cricket! They were the reason why we failed to bring back the Ashes I had so much joy in helping to win out there four years earlier. Their catching also helped considerably. It was magnificent. Greg Chappell, Ashley Mallett and Ian Redpath all brought off some superb catches they had no right to smell let alone get a hand to. Throughout, the Australians were a wonderful sight in the field with their catching, running and throwing. I'm afraid we looked a poor second best in that department.

The difference Lillee and Thomson made can be seen from just one glance at the scorebook for the final Test in Melbourne when we won so easily after scoring 529 in our first innings through a fine innings of 188 by Mike Denness, 146 from Keith Fletcher and Tony Greig slashing his way around for 89 in two hours. Thomson was missing through injury, Lillee put out of the match after injuring his foot during his opening spell.

Without Lillee and Thomson – or even with just one of them – I think we could have brought the Ashes back. As it was I believe the series was closer than the 4-1 result suggests. Perhaps we may not quite have deserved to have been level pegging at 2-2 after five Test matches but that might have easily been the case if we had had the breaks as we did in the West Indies 12 months earlier.

We were well beaten in the opening Test in Brisbane when Thomson surprised us on an underprepared wicket following heavy rain. He really was a revelation in that match. He had looked nothing special in the State game against Queensland the week before.

Our confidence, too, was high when the match started after a successful warming up period during which we had won two matches against State sides and been on the right side in draws against two more. After Thomson and Lillee, we never really recaptured that confidence.

We couldn't have had a better start to the match either when Australia batted first and we had Ian Redpath and Wally Edwards out for only 10. Then Ian and Greg Chappell took over and we gradually slid out of the game in losing by 166 runs.

I have three distinct memories of that match. The frustration of watching Australian bowler Max Walker come in at number ten and stay around for 41 runs – something he was to do time and time again during the series. So often he and the other tail-enders were able to give the Australians another 100 runs more than anybody expected, allowing Chappell to keep attacking fields when it came to our turn to bat. Perhaps this is a criticism of our bowlers and our lack of penetration when trying to dismiss the tail.

Another memory is of the duel between Greig and the Australian fast bowlers when he made 110 in our first innings. And of one moment in particular when Lillee bowled him a bouncer. Greig's response was to make out he was attempting to head the ball away football style. Lillee was not amused. He bounded in furiously next ball but somehow Greig got on the front foot, hit the ball on the up and smashed it through the covers for four. Greig was signalling a boundary long before the ball hit the fence. That was one up to him.

The other memories are painful ones. Being hit in the chest by Lillee in our first innings and being hit on the hand by Thomson in the second. That was the time Thomson came to life with his match winning six for 46 which set him on the road to glory.

We were well beaten in the second Test match at Perth when Colin Cowdrey bravely stepped in having been flown out from England to help our injury situation. The decision to invite Colin as a replacement at the age of 42 gave birth to a number of fun poking cartoons and insulting comments in the Australian press but we were right behind the decision. He is still a wonderful player of fast bowling. He was tremendous in Perth as was Fred Titmus with the bat. Colin was hit a number of times but he never flinched, still got into line and frequently played his strokes with time to spare. He didn't score the weight of runs he hoped but his influence on the others around him as well as his experience was invaluable.

We lost that match by nine wickets inside four days and the tour seemed to be slipping by and away from us. But then it almost turned our way. The third Test played in front of more than a quarter of a million spectators at Melbourne – almost 78,000 watched the first day – was drawn. The Australians will say they finished just eight runs short of victory.

I must admit they have a point, but we were only two wickets away from victory. I came on to bowl one of the most crucial overs of my career – the penultimate over – with Australia needing 14 runs to win, Walker and Lillee at the wicket and two batsmen to come.

Lillee was at the other end. I dare not let him score more than two off the over. One loose ball and a four would almost certainly let Australia in for victory. I kept everything well pitched up forcing Lillee to play straight, willing to concede a single to mid-on or mid-off but nothing more. In the end I managed a maiden. Seven runs came off the final over when Lillee was out having a smear and the game ended in a draw.

I think we could have won that one with a little bit more luck and confidence. Australia had started the day needing 242 to win with all their wickets in hand but were soon in trouble losing Ross and Wally Edwards with only five on the board. We were handicapped by losing Mike Hendrick with ham-string trouble but I felt we let that match get away. The series could have been 2-1 to Australia at that stage.

We lost the next at Sydney and that was another disappointment. We were beaten by 171 runs when Denness stood down and John Edrich took over the captaincy. There was never any question of us winning the match but I thought we should have saved it. We started the last day with all our wickets intact but couldn't play out the six hours. There were only 43 balls to go when Geoff Arnold was caught off Mallett and Australia had regained the Ashes.

With four Tests gone we were three down and had lost the Ashes. It should have been only 2-1 down with the Ashes still to fight for. And the series all square after that fifth Test at Adelaide when we caught them on a rain affected wicket.

Within half an hour of the start I was bowling and I finished with seven for 113, my best figures overseas in a Test match. At one stage I had taken all seven. At another I had a spell of five for 12 off 45 deliveries when it was really turning. At one time Australia were 84 for five wickets having lost McCosker, Redpath, the Chappell brothers and Marsh. Amazing it all slipped away from us after lunch on that opening day and they totalled 304. It should have been our day but it belonged to Australia yet again. Our confidence was at a low ebb. The disappointment was too much for all of us and we lost that match without any trouble. It was the low part of the tour as far as I was concerned although I'd come out of the Test with 11 wickets.

With just a little more solidarity in our middle order batting, the series could have gone so differently despite the presence of Lillee and Thomson. There wasn't that much separating the sides and we were always under the handicap of a series of injuries.

I came away from Australia under the impression they have little to offer outside their 13 or 14 Test players. We saw very little to get excited about in the way of new talent when playing against the State sides. The gap between their State cricket and Test cricket is much greater than our County and Test cricket.

In many ways it was not such a tough and demanding tour as when we won the Ashes five years earlier in a nail biting finish. With the Ashes gone early, there was less tension involved in the games over the last six weeks or so. Nor was there any sniping at each other which could so easily have happened after the run of defeats. Alec Bedser saw to that. I thought he was an extremely fine Manager who kept everybody on an even keel.

Although I had known him as a Selector since 1966, I have never really got to know him. Sadly, it is not often that selectors and players get together. Only at pre-Test dinners. I got to know him on that tour. So did the other players. He got to know us too and how we feel and react. I think it could have an important bearing on the future of our cricket.

We had a good many laughs on the tour, David Lloyd so frequently stealing the limelight. One day he came in having fended Lillee and Thomson off for a couple of hours, sat down and pretended to write a letter home. His letter started 'Dear Mum, I received a half volley today . . . in the nets . . . I didn't know what to do with it.'

I wasn't too impressed by the Aussie crowds in general. They, not Lillee and Thomson, seemed to be thirsting for blood. They were delighted when anybody was hit and tried their hardest to work the bowlers up into a bouncer pitching frenzy. Many times they chanted 'Lillee, Lillee, Lillee' the chant getting louder and louder as he approached the wicket. The other frequent chant was 'Ashes to Ashes, Dust to Dust, if Thomson don't get you then Lillee must'. And so it went on. As for the poor fielders, myself included, who fielded on the fence, the abuse we sometimes received, had to be heard to be believed.

I was fortunate enough to take 40 wickets on the tour of

Australia, 25 of them being captured in Adelaide. What was disappointing on analysing my Test record out there was that 11 of my 17 Test wickets were taken in Adelaide, leaving only six Test wickets in the other four Tests I played. I was rather disappointed at this. One thing I did miss was not working in harness with my spinning partner. Very frequently I seemed to operate with a quick bowler the other end, Fred Titmus or Tony Greig coming on my end, when I tired, preference of wind or breeze always being given to the seamers.

One final thought about the tour. The unfortunate accident involving New Zealander Ewan Chatfield. I shall never forget our dressing-room after it happened. A few of us had a stiff whisky as an atmosphere of gloom, sadness and shame hung over us. I was sharing a room with Peter Lever and I've never known anybody more upset. Chatfield had stopped breathing. There is no doubt physiotherapist Bernard Thomas saved his life. And that sets me wondering. How well are we equipped in this country if the same thing should happen over here? It could happen so easily on a deserted ground during a county match. It will do so some day before crash helmets come in. Will there always be a Bernard Thomas around? A sobering thought.

THE UNDERWOOD FILE
Compiled by Bill Frindall

Full names:	Derek Leslie UNDERWOOD
Date and place of birth:	8 June 1945 Bromley, Kent
Place of education:	Beckenham and Penge Grammar School
Height:	6 ft 0 in
Batting and bowling type:	Right Hand Bat, Left Arm Medium/ Slow Left Arm.

Career Record – All First-Class Matches:

Figures do not include the 1974/75 MCC tour to Australia.

BATTING AND FIELDING **Not out*

Season	*M*	*I*	*NO*	*HS*	*Runs*	*Av*	50	*Ct*
1963	27	30	11	24	210	11.05	—	12
1964	29	31	7	33	179	7.45	—	8
1965	31	37	8	27	138	4.75	—	8
1966	29	33	10	21*	154	6.69	—	17
1966–67	6	5	1	12	22	5.50	—	3
1967	27	26	4	47	210	9.54	—	16
1967–68	2	2	1	0*	0	0.00	—	3
1968	29	33	8	45*	280	11.20	—	9
1968–69	6	4	0	22	35	8.75	—	—
1969	24	27	4	80	234	10.17	1	9
1969–70	4	5	0	37	46	9.20	—	1
1970	21	23	6	32	147	8.64	—	10
1970–71	13	14	7	13*	41	5.85	—	11
1971	25	28	6	34	260	11.81	—	11
1972	18	19	7	23*	120	10.00	—	6
1972–73	10	8	4	20*	55	13.75	—	4
1973	20	17	3	23	110	7.85	—	9
1973–74	7	10	3	24	100	14.28	—	5
1974	16	16	5	43	116	10.54	—	7
Totals	344	368	95	(80)	2,457	9.00	1	149

Highest score: 80 Kent v Lancashire at Old Trafford, Manchester in 1969.

BOWLING † *8-ball overs.*

Season	*O*	*M*	*R*	*W*	*Av*	*5wI*	*10wM*
1963	941.4	376	2,134	101	21.12	3	1
1964	1,069.3	428	2,450	101	24.25	5	1
1965	982.4	423	2,259	89	25.38	6	1
1966	1,104.5	475	2,167	157	13.80	13	5
1966–67	245	102	406	13	31.23	—	—
1967	979.1	459	1,686	136	12.39	14	4
1967–68	77.4	43	96	24	4.00	3	1
1968	957.4	435	1,821	123	14.80	6	3
1968–69	187	71	380	20	19.00	2	—
1969	808.3	355	1,561	101	15.45	8	2
1969–70	146	62	275	11	25.00	—	—
1970	851.2	307	2,043	89	22.95	7	2
1970–71	422†	110	1,123	43	26.11	3	1
1971	945.5	368	1,986	102	19.47	7	2
1972	652.4	227	1,485	71	20.91	3	2
1972–73	442.5	164	934	26	35.92	—	—
1973	590.2	219	1,363	49	27.81	3	1
1973–74	263.5	88	573	12	47.75	—	—
1974	563	229	1,181	65	18.16	7	3
Totals	11,809.3 +422†	4,941	25,923	1,333	19.44	90	29

Best innings analysis: 9 for 28 Kent v Sussex at Hastings in 1964
Best match analysis: 15 for 43 International XI v President's XI at Colombo, Ceylon in 1967–68.
Balls per wicket: 55.68. Runs per 100 balls: 34.92.

Underwood has taken five or more wickets in an innings on 90 occasions, 69 of them for Kent in county championship matches. Contrary to criticism that he is a far greater wicket-taking force on Kent pitches than on those outside the county, it can be seen from the following chart that 34 of those instances (49.3%) have been achieved in away matches.

Five or more wickets in an innings in Championship Matches

Home (35)	*Opponents*	*Away* (34)
6–54 (68); 6–75 (74)	D	
6–20 (66); 5–68 (69)	E	6–26 (65); 9–37 (66); 6–45 (69)
5–45, 6–28 (67); 5–76 (71)	Gm	7–25 (68)
6–52 (66); 6–38, 6–42 (74)	Gs	6–68, 5–82 (70)
7–35, 5–15 (67); 7–17 (68); 5–35 (71)	H	
6–28 (67)	La	6–9 (66); 5–66 (71)
5–23 (66); 6–58 (70)	Le	5–50 (63); 7–33(67); 6–67 (72)
5–86 (70)	M	5–71 (65); 5–29, 5–58 (66); 6–22 (69)
6–43 (64); 6–72 (67); 5–54	Nh	5–75 (73)
(68)	Nt	5–28 (66)
5–71 (65); 7–46 (68); 5–20 (69)	Sm	5–55, 6–78 (66); 5–40 (70)
6–88 (63); 6–99 (65); 6–44	Sy	5–57 (66); 5–59 (67)
(74); 6–18 (71)	Sx	9–28 (64); 7–38, 7–44 (67); 5–43, 8–9 (73)
7–103, 7–110 (70)	Wa	6–39 (64); 5–70, 6–51 (65)
7–50 (66); 5–24 (67)	Wo	5–25 (74)
5–19, 5–41 (71)	Y	7–97 (64); 7–30 (66); 7–28 (71); 8–70 (72)

Similarly, 12 of the 22 instances of his claiming ten or more wickets in championship matches have occurred outside Kent.

Ten or more wickets in Championship Matches

Home (10)	*Opponents*	*Away* (12)
	D	
	E	13–57 (66)
11–73 (67)	Gm	11–62 (68)
12–80 (74)	Gs	11–150 (70)
12–50 (67); 11–64 (68)	H	
	La	10–68 (66)
	Le	
	M	10–87 (66)
	Nh	
	Nt	
11–146 (68)	Sm	11–133 (66)
10–113 (63); 10–116 (74)	Sy	
10–66 (71)	Sx	11–74 (64); 14–82 (67); 13–52 (73)
14–213 (70)	Wa	11–121 (65)
	Wo	
10–60 (71)	Y	11–135 (66); 11–96 (72)

Career Record – Test Matches

BATTING AND FIELDING *Not out

Season	*Opponents*	*M*	*I*	*NO*	*HS*	*Runs*	*Av*	*Ct*
1966	West Indies	2	4	2	12*	22	11.00	2
1967	Pakistan	2	1	1	2*	2	—	1
1968	Australia	4	4	4	45*	69	—	2
1968–69	Pakistan	3	3	0	22	28	9.33	—
1969	West Indies	2	3	1	16	31	15.50	3
1969	New Zealand	3	4	0	16	24	6.00	1
1970	Rest of World	3	5	0	19	29	5.80	4
1970–71	Australia	5	6	3	8*	16	5.33	4
1970–71	New Zealand	2	3	3	8*	9	—	3
1971	Pakistan	1	1	1	9*	9	—	1
1971	India	1	2	0	22	33	16.50	1
1972	Australia	2	3	2	5	8	8.00	—
1972–73	India	4	5	1	9	19	4.75	3
1972–73	Pakistan	2	2	2	20*	25	—	—
1973	New Zealand	1	1	1	20*	20	—	—
1973	West Indies	3	5	0	14	35	7.00	2
1973–74	West Indies	4	7	3	24	67	16.75	2
1974	India	3	3	0	9	25	8.33	2
1974	Pakistan	3	3	1	43	64	32.00	—
Totals		50	65	25	(45*)	535	13.37	31

Highest score: 45* v Australia at Headingley, Leeds in 1968.

BOWLING

Season	*Opponents*	*Balls*	*M*	*R*	*W*	*Av*	*5wI*	*10wM*
1966	West Indies	414	25	172	1	172.00	—	—
1967	Pakistan	396	27	129	8	16.12	1	—
1968	Australia	1,259	103	302	20	15.10	1	—
1968–69	Pakistan	636	40	204	8	25.50	1	—
1969	West Indies	318	29	101	6	16.83	—	—
1969	New Zealand	900	70	220	24	9.16	3	2
1970	Rest of World	719	44	283	7	40.42	—	—
1970–71	Australia	1,558	50	520	16	32.50	—	—
1970–71	New Zealand	673	28	205	17	12.05	3	1
1971	Pakistan	246	13	102	0	—	—	—
1971	India	378	20	121	4	30.25	—	—
1972	Australia	750	49	266	16	16.62	1	1
1972–73	India	1,288	82	457	15	30.46	—	—
1972–73	Pakistan	576	35	215	3	71.66	—	—
1973	New Zealand	108	6	41	0	—	—	—
1973	West Indies	798	38	330	8	41.25	—	—
1973–74	West Indies	827	45	314	5	62.80	—	—
1974	India	402	25	146	4	36.50	—	—
1974	Pakistan	683	48	218	17	12.82	2	1
Totals		12,929	777	4,346	179	24.27	12	5

Best innings analysis: 8 for 51 } v Pakistan at Lord's in 1974.
Best match analysis: 13 for 71 }
Balls per wicket: 72.22. Runs per 100 balls: 33.61.

Bowling Record Against Each Country

Country	*Tests*	*Balls*	*M*	*R*	*W*	*Av*	*5wI*	*10wM*
Australia	11	3,567	202	1,088	52	20.92	2	1
West Indies	11	2,357	137	917	20	45.85	—	—
New Zealand	6	1,681	104	466	41	11.36	6	3
India	8	2,068	127	724	23	31.47	—	—
Pakistan	11	2,537	163	868	36	24.11	4	1

Career Record—Limited-Overs Matches

BATTING AND FIELDING *Not out

Competition	*M*	*I*	*NO*	*Runs*	*Av*	*Ct*
Gillette Cup	28	18	4	105	7.50	11
John Player League	72	31	14	156	9.17	18
Benson and Hedges Cup	15	8	3	47	9.40	5
Fenner Trophy	4	4	2	27	13.50	3
Prudential Trophy	6	3	2	19	19.00	—
Totals	125	64	25	354	9.07	37

Highest Scores

Gillette Cup	28	Kent v Sussex	Tunbridge Wells	1963
John Player League	22	Kent v Worcester-shire	Dudley	1969
Benson and Hedges Cup	17	Kent v Essex	Canterbury	1973
Fenner Trophy	11*	Kent v Lancashire	Scarborough	1972
Prudential Trophy	17	England v Pakistan	Birmingham	1974

BOWLING

Competition	*O*	*M*	*R*	*W*	*Av*	*4w*	*R/Over*
Gillette Cup	292.4	67	979	40	24.47	1	3.34
John Player League†	496.2	74	1,803	133	13.55	14	3.63
Benson and Hedges Cup	151.4	32	441	18	24.50	—	2.90
Fenner Trophy	40	8	137	10	13.70	1	3.42
Prudential Trophy	51	6	169	7	24.14	—	3.31
Totals	1,031.4	187	3,529	208	16.96	16	3.42

Best Analyses

Gillette Cup	4 for 57		
	Kent v Leicestershire	Canterbury	1974
John Player League	5 for 19		
	Kent v Gloucestershire	Maidstone	1972
Benson and Hedges Cup	2 for 14		
	Kent v Cambridge U.	Cambridge	1974
Fenner Trophy	5 for 36		
	Kent v Lancashire	Scarborough	1972
Prudential Trophy	3 for 30		
	England v West Indies	Leeds	1973

† Only K. D. Boyce (139) has taken more wickets in this competition and no other bowler approaches Underwood's record of 14 shares in the annual £1,000 bowlers' pool.

Career Highlights

1963 Made début in first-class cricket for Kent v Yorkshire at Hull when aged 17 years 11 months, scoring 10 and returning analyses of 21–6–40–4 and 3–2–2–1.
Became the eleventh and youngest bowler to take 100 wickets in the season of his first-class debut.

1964 Took 9 for 28 v Sussex at Hastings – his best analysis.
Awarded County Cap when aged 19; the second-youngest Kent player after M. C. Cowdrey.

1966 Took 9 for 37 v Essex at Westcliff-on-Sea.
First bowler to take 100 wickets in 1966 – on 28 July.
Made England début in Test cricket v West Indies at Nottingham when aged 21 years 23 days and shared in record England 10th wicket partnership v West Indies: 65 with B. L. d'Oliveira.
Headed national bowling averages with most wickets (157, average 13.80)—the first Kent bowler to do so since Colin Blythe in 1914.
Elected 'Young Cricketer of the Year' by the Cricket Writers' Club.

1967 Toured Pakistan with MCC under-25 team.
First bowler to take 100 wickets in 1967 – on 30 July.
Headed national bowling averages for second successive year with 136 wickets, average 12.39.

1968 Toured Africa and the Far East with J. Lister's International XI and took 8 for 10 and 7 for 33 v President's XI at Colombo.
Scored 45 not out in 52 minutes v Australia at Leeds; his highest score in Test cricket and the highest by an England number eleven against Australia.
Bowled England to victory in the Fifth Test at The Oval, taking 7 for 50 including the final wicket with just six minutes to spare.
One of *Wisden's* 'Five Cricketers of 1968'.
Selected for (later cancelled) MCC tour of South Africa.

1969 Toured Pakistan and Ceylon with MCC.
Scored maiden fifty (80) v Lancashire at Manchester, going in as 'nightwatchman', staying over four hours and making top score in Kent's total of 198.
Took 7 for 32 v New Zealand at Lord's; the best analysis for either country in England–New Zealand Tests.

1970 Toured the West Indies with the International Cavaliers and Duke of Norfolk's XI.
Took the wickets of C. Inman, R. Illingworth and R. W. Tolchard in 4 balls for Kent v Leicestershire at Leicester.
Toured Australia and New Zealand with MCC, taking 3 for 0 in First Test at Brisbane and sharing in match-saving 9th wicket partnership of 116 unbroken with B. L. d'Oliveira v South Australia at Adelaide.

1971 Took his 1000th first-class wicket in the First Test v New Zealand at Christchurch – his 247th match and when aged 25 years 264 days. Only W. Rhodes (in 1902) and G. A. Lohmann (in 1890) achieved this feat at an earlier age. In the same match – his 35th Test – he took his 100th wicket for England.

1972 Toured India, Sri Lanka and Pakistan with MCC.

1973 Shared in record 10th wicket partnership for England v Pakistan – 55 with P. I. Pocock at Hyderabad.
Returned the best first-class analysis of 1973 – 10.1–6–9–8 v Sussex at Hastings.

1974 Toured West Indies and Bermuda with MCC.
Took 8 for 51 (13 for 71 in the match) v Pakistan at Lord's; his best innings and match analyses in Test matches; the best England analysis since J. C. Laker's 10 for 53 in 1956, and record innings and match analyses in England–Pakistan Tests.
Shared in 2nd wicket partnership of 129 with D. L. Amiss, going in as 'nightwatchman' v Pakistan at The Oval and scoring 43 in 184 minutes – his longest innings in Test cricket.

INDEX

compiled by Penny Phipps